Quantifiably Better

Delivering HR Analytics from Start to Finish

Steve VanWieren

Technics Publications

Published by:

2 Lindsley Road
Basking Ridge, NJ 07920 USA

https://www.TechnicsPub.com

Cover design by Lorena Molinari

Edited by Lauren McCafferty

First Printing 2017
Copyright © 2017 by Steve VanWieren

ISBN, print ed.	9781634622219
ISBN, Kindle ed.	9781634622226
ISBN, ePub ed.	9781634622233
ISBN, PDF ed.	9781634622240

Library of Congress Control Number: 2017933052

Contents

Acknowledgements

I wish to first thank my heavenly Father for giving me the opportunity to serve so many people over my career, which led to this book.

I want to thank the love of my life, Starla, for putting up with my strange love of numbers, as well as all of my shortcomings. Your love is what keeps me going each and every day.

I thank my daughters, Chaney, Grace, and Becca, for never forgetting that every day you laugh and cry is a good day.

I would also like to thank my mother and late father, who gave me unconditional support my entire life, as well as a really great childhood.

To my brother, Jon, and my best friend, Glenn, for forcing me at a young age to invent baseball simulation games. You two are probably more responsible for my love of numbers than just about anyone.

I am thankful for all of my bosses, co-workers, peers, business partners, teachers, classmates, students, friends, and customers, who really provided the experiences that I used throughout the book. I'd especially like to thank my own direct reports over the years for being part of my own experiments, and I am hopeful that they learned as much from me as I did from them.

I'd like to specifically thank Judy Glick-Smith for connecting me with Steve Hoberman, and I'd like to thank Steve and his team for all of their help in helping me get this book to market, as it was an entirely new experience for me.

Finally, to all of the other authors out there, I have a totally different respect for you than I did before attempting to write this. I can definitely admit that I underestimated the difficulty involved. You have my admiration forever going forward.

Introduction

Before I get too deep into the background of "Quantifiably Better", I want to put one data point out on the table.

Up to this point, the total # of books I have written is zero (0).

When I decided to embark on this journey to write a professional book, I had a really strong game plan for how I was going to do it. Write 2,000 words a day. No more than 10 chapters, as it needs to be consumable. Be done in a few weeks. I had a good outline, and I have tons of experience as a public speaker and blogger, so I felt I would do pretty well at this exercise. I knew the style of writing I wanted to use would apply to my target audience of HR leaders. Everything was lined up and ready to go.

The first day, I wrote almost 2,500 words, and I felt great. The next day, I read what I had written the previous day, and I became worried very quickly. It wasn't very good. I went back and re-wrote most of the chapter, and I repeated the exercise of rereading what I had written the next day. My worries turned into fully-fledged fear. It still wasn't very good. It would have been very easy to give up at that point, as my life would certainly have been easier if I didn't put this own pressure on myself. It was, after all, a *choice* to write it. I started to realize that I had a measurable outcome I wanted to achieve.

I wanted the total # of books I had written to increase to one (1).

I am a very data-driven person, and having a simple metric staring at me every day revealing that the total # of books I had written was still zero (0) was all the motivation I needed to keep going. Oddly enough, this little anecdote begins to explain the purpose of the book.

I started to apply the very principles that were in my outline, and I began to make real progress. I realized that the methodology that is contained in this book works for just about anything. That got my creative juices flowing.

That brings me to the history of who I am and the background of this book. The phrase "quantifiably better" came to me many years ago, when I was writing a vision statement for one of my jobs. I felt that these two words exemplified not only the goals of the group, but also who I was at many levels.

I grew up crunching baseball numbers. My late father was a broadcaster for the Atlanta Braves for 33 years. He used to bring home his scorebooks once they were filled up, and my older brother (Jon), my best friend (Glenn), and I would invent games using them. I was probably 7 years old when I started down the path of simulating baseball statistics. Not many 7-year old kids have that on their resume.

Baseball statistics could be found almost anywhere for a 7-year old. I could find them on the backs of baseball cards, which I used to buy for a dime a pack at the local convenience store. I could find them in box scores in newspapers. Even though I was still learning to read, I understood that when stats were collected on players, the knowledge about how well they were performing was accumulating. The more information, the better.

In addition, my father had row after row of baseball history books in his library. Shelf upon shelf was full of baseball knowledge, and I consumed it like crazy. Sure, I also played little league, but I was more interested in keeping the stats on myself and teammates to see how we compared with historical major leaguers than actually trying to improve my own game.

I would come up with ways to simulate players and seasons, often over entire careers. I would make fictional trades between teams. I discovered board games like APBA (American Professional Baseball Association), which took baseball simulation to a whole new level for me. I would even invent players using names from the phone book, using the historical player stats from my father's books as guidance for how players should really perform - it had to be realistic, of course.

Once the PC became a thing, my older brother learned to program so we could do things through the computer instead of with scorebooks, baseball cards, and dice. The three of us would stay up until the wee hours of the night simulating baseball statistics with the computer. It became such a huge part of my daily life that I sometimes would think it was the fictional year instead of the actual year.

This probably sounds like an addiction to you, and maybe it was or still is. After all, I still love crunching baseball numbers. But keep in mind, at this point, I was a high schooler. Even worse, I recognized something was missing.

Despite my best efforts, I noticed over time that real players would have ups and downs. They would peak at certain points of their careers, and skills would deteriorate later in their careers. None of the simulators I had created or played accounted for any of these situations. I tried various approaches using my gut, but nothing was realistic. I wasn't sure what to do next.

When I got to college and took my first statistics class, I started to realize that I could actually simulate better baseball results if I was able to apply the new techniques I was learning. I kind of fell in love with Statistics at that point, and I ended up getting both a BS and an MS in Statistics from the University of Georgia. Go Dawgs.

What was interesting though was that I wasn't just learning new techniques. I already understood my data pretty well with my general knowledge of baseball. So, I was thinking about the application of statistics before any of my classmates. I wrote every paper and thesis on baseball numbers in some form. I cannot begin to explain how much this helped me throughout my entire career.

As I entered the working world, I got to apply these techniques across all kinds of domains, from healthcare to financial services and eventually to people. I touched hundreds of data sources, and led all kinds of groups and functions, teaching companies to take steps forward that were based on empirical evidence rather than gut feel.

Once I got to working with data about people, I fell in love with it - the same kind of love that I have for baseball statistics. I consumed information like crazy. I read articles, books, and blogs. I started to read what psychologists wrote. I spoke with brain surgeons about how the brain works. I took dozens of personality tests, looking for any new nuggets of information.

I studied the data that was available about employees, looking for any kinds of patterns that others may have overlooked. I spoke with hundreds of HR leaders and consumers about their challenges, and I taught them better ways to measure things.

I started to see articles as more academic, introducing excellent new knowledge and data points to consider, but rarely solutions. I especially questioned those that shared results from surveys and surveys alone, never actually tying the survey results to anything that would interest a CEO. I realized that very few companies out there really had good measurements about their people.

No wonder turnover is such a problem. HR leaders are being asked to lead efforts to reduce turnover, and they are most likely throwing a single drop of water at a fire that requires a hose attached to an endless stream. As I became more familiar with the challenges that HR leaders were truly dealing with, I started to apply my knowledge of data and analytics to helping solve their daily challenges. The more data I had, the greater opportunity I saw to make a difference.

But, as I spoke with HR leaders all over North America, I began to realize that they were often stuck in a situation where it was going to be difficult or even impossible to take a step towards becoming data-driven. Many didn't know where to start, and those that had started didn't know where to go next.

I realized that they needed a resource they could use during all phases of the data and analytics experience. I knew my skillset was unique, and I felt I could help. So, I decided to write this book. My hope is that it will help you understand how to get started. If you have already started, then I hope it will help you think outside the box to continually challenge yourself. I wrote this book for you more than me because we all have an opportunity to make things better in our own lives and the lives of our employees. We can make things better.

Quantifiably better.

So now I have the thrill of announcing a change in my own data point. The # of books I have now written is one (1).

You also have a new data point. The # of times you have read this book is zero (0). I look forward to talking with anyone who increases their own metric to at least one (1).

CHAPTER 1
One Less Thing

There are lots of memorable quotes from the movie *Forrest Gump*.[1] "Life is like a box of chocolates." "You never know what you're gonna get." "Stupid is as stupid does."

One that may not be quite as memorable to many is actually one of the more important principles behind the concept of *Quantifiably Better*. It involves a scene where Forrest is sitting at the bus stop sharing his story:

"Lieutenant Dan got me to invest in some kind of fruit company [referring to Apple]. So, then I got a call from him, saying we don't have to worry about money no more. And I said, that's good! One less thing." - Forrest Gump

One less thing. Such a simple principle. It is one that most of us are living by unknowingly every day. We don't have to think too hard about how to bathe, drive a car, ride a bike, walk, read, write, or count things. Once we have these skills, we don't have to worry about them anymore. I say, that's good! One less thing!

In the last few years, the usage of data and analytics to help make business decisions has exploded. Sites like Forbes.com have entire sections of their websites dedicated to articles on data-driven business. Harvard Business Review named the role of data scientist as the "sexiest job of the 21st century".[2] In just about every article you read, you will find a peppering of data points and measures.

Data and analytics is simply everywhere now - from measuring how many steps you take each day to monitoring sentiment in your social media postings. Businesses and organizations of all kinds are learning that data-driven decision making often trumps "gut feel."

Yet there are still industries and areas of expertise that have yet to leverage analytics to their full capacity. HR departments are one such example. They are trailing other business areas, such as sales, marketing, and operations, when it comes to data-driven decision making. HR leaders, managers, and employees all have the opportunity to figure out better ways to leverage these new capabilities. Getting started does not have to be intimidating.

Do Whatever it Takes

To introduce this concept, let's consider the most basic of examples.

Think about what a child goes through when learning to eat with a fork. The child has one main problem to solve: she is hungry. The usual manner in which she resolves her hunger is to eat with her hands. But she knows that while eating with her hands resolves her hunger issue, there is a secondary problem: when she eats with her hands, she ends up being messy. She doesn't like it when she has to be cleaned up. She knows that her parents don't eat with their hands - they use special tools.

Then one day, she is given one of these tools - a fork. She is also given the opportunity to use the fork all by herself, which is a new responsibility. In the past, someone else has always held the fork. This time, she has to try to use the fork for herself. She has seen her parents and siblings use a fork successfully before, and she wants to be more like them. She doesn't know how to use it perfectly, but she gets a little training from her parents on how to hold it and stab food with it.

Despite her best efforts on day 1, she fails miserably. She tries to poke the food, but it keeps missing the fork, doesn't stay attached, or - *gulp* - falls to the floor, and the dog eats it instead. The child decides that the fork is useless, and she goes back to the way she has always done it, and she eats with her hands. The next day, her parents give her food and a fork once again. She gives it another shot, and this time, while still imperfect, she successfully gets food on the fork a few times. She even gets a few bites into her mouth.

Over time, using the fork becomes easier and easier, and soon, she is no longer using her hands to eat. Her behavior is changed; now, she and her parents no longer have to deal with the clean-up exercise.

The child probably isn't thinking about how she achieved success. But there were very simple steps that were involved:

- There were two essential items that were given to the child: food and a fork.

- The child understood what happens with food (it solves her hunger) and the fork (gets the food to her mouth).

- She tried over and over to use the tool to feed herself until she no longer needed to think about it.

At some point, the child instinctively knows what to do when food is placed in front of her and a fork is nearby. Her brain automatically knows what to do next.

FEEDING YOURSELF SMARTLY

The example demonstrates how a common task such as eating was totally reinvented for the child. She knew what she wanted to do, but she was probably a little bit afraid to try it. She was frustrated when she didn't get results right away. But her persistence eventually caused the desired outcome to be achieved.

When applying this same logic to data and analytics, all you really need to learn is how to solve your problems a little differently —eat with the "analytics fork". You will likely go through the same feelings as the child in the example: you know what you want to do, you might try something and achieve success right away, or you may fail. Or you may be too afraid or frustrated with not obtaining the desired outcome right away.

But much like the child eating with the fork, persistence with data and analytics can yield the desired outcome. It just takes practice.

THE DATA-INSIGHT-ACTION CYCLE

In general, there is a pretty basic way of understanding how problems of any kind are solved:

1. DATA is collected and available

2. INSIGHT about the DATA is obtainable

3. ACTION is taken based on the INSIGHT

Not every problem is as simple to solve as learning to eat with a fork. The ramifications of messing up are small in that case. Going back to the old way of eating with one's hands does not cause any obvious financial burden on one's family, for instance.

For HR professionals, this becomes a little bit more challenging. You are dealing with compliance issues, reducing costs of benefits, hiring smarter and faster, and making sure your employees are getting paid the correct amounts. You know there are some key issues to resolve, like reducing turnover, or improving the company culture, but there aren't obvious paths of success. What happens frequently is that *fear of change* defeats the *opportunity to change*. But it doesn't have to.

In our example, the child was definitely afraid, but she had everything she needed to obtain success.

- DATA: food, fork

- INSIGHT: food solves hunger; fork solves messiness

- ACTION: poke food, move fork to mouth, pull food off fork with mouth; repeat until perfected

She had everything she needed in DATA, INSIGHT, and ACTION to change her behavior and meet the desired goals.

If you really break the fork-training scenario down in analytic terms, the goal was actually to improve the time in which food could be attached and placed into the mouth. Once the child got to an "acceptable" level, she didn't need to keep improving it. At some point, the time was "fast enough".

If her parents were truly geeky, they could have timed each attempt, and measured the improvement. Even if they didn't know what the optimal outcome was, they would have been able to show improvement from day 1 until she was successful. Her chart might look something like the one shown in Figure 1.1.

The child probably didn't know she had reached an optimal stage after day 5, but the data shows otherwise. The parents could probably see that by day 5, the child was eating just like them with a fork.

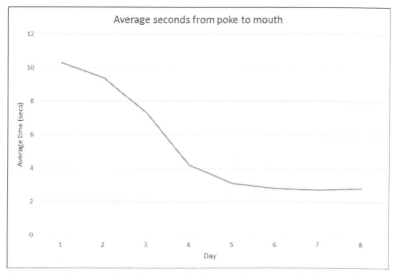

Figure 1.1: Average time in seconds from poke to mouth (by day)

Does that mean that the child was an expert? Of course not! One can imagine that the same geeky parents continued to capture the data going forward, measuring the results in months or years instead of days and found continued improvement when looking at it more broadly. Figure 1.2 on the facing page demonstrates this.

In changing the X-axis, the parents might see that the child continued to improve over time. Maybe she reached an apex of improvement in month 7. Or perhaps there is continued improvement to come. Maybe if that metric gets too low, it has an adverse effect; perhaps the child begins to eat too fast and gains weight.

NOTE: Despite my geekiness, this is all made up data. I taught my kids to eat with a fork just like every other parent. I would bet, though, that this is what it might look like.

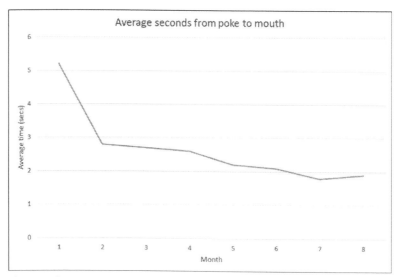

Figure 1.2: Average seconds from poke to mouth (by month)

Each section of the DATA-INSIGHT-ACTION philosophy has techniques to measure effectiveness. That is why the process is so successful. Each section is measurable in different ways, and as a result, HR leaders can start with the basics and work into solving more complex problems as they go.

For example, DATA itself needs to be measured to ensure the quality of the information is good. If the quality of the information is good, then the INSIGHT obtained from the DATA can be trusted. ACTION needs to be properly captured or recorded as DATA, so that it can be converted into INSIGHT as well. Finally, you can gain INSIGHT into understanding whether the ACTION produces the desired result. The three things actually flow together in a cycle, as shown in Figure 1.3.

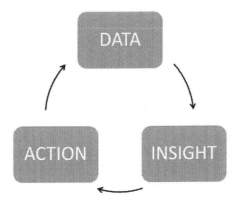

Figure 1.3: DATA-INSIGHT-ACTION cycle

Quantifiably Better will cover in detail each step of the cycle.

DATA

- Understanding your data

- Manipulating your data

INSIGHT

- Monitoring your data

ACTION

- Preparing for action

- Purpose-driven action

- Experimenting with action

I'll also share some challenges that you will likely encounter during this journey, and how you can best be prepared for them.

IT WORKS FOR ALL KINDS OF PROBLEMS

This simple three-tier process may seem rudimentary, but it is the way that the brain solves problems. Not just simple, elementary tasks that a child learns, like eating with a fork, but real grown-up problems that require much more sophisticated intelligence. Thankfully, it has been proven that the brain rapidly adapts when it receives new knowledge.[3] In other words, once the brain receives new information and intelligence, it quickly changes its old way of thinking to something new. The end result is a change in behavior.

One goal of *Quantifiably Better* is to change human behavior by using this same philosophy, simply by making things measurable. It is about taking the hardest HR problems for CEOs, HR leaders, managers, and employees, and finding a way to make progress. Not just any progress - *measurable* progress.

When you actually *can* measure something, you are far more likely to make a breakthrough on the problem you are trying to solve. William Thomson, the Scottish physicist known as Lord Kelvin, described it this way:

"I often say that when you can measure what you are speaking about, and express it in numbers, you know something about it; but when you cannot express it in numbers, your knowledge is of a meagre and unsatisfactory kind; it may be the beginning of knowledge, but you have scarcely, in your thoughts, advanced to the stage of science, whatever the matter may be."[4]

In other words, "gut feel" isn't scientific. But using the DATA-INSIGHT-ACTION cycle is.

The approach can be used to improve easily measured things like financial outcomes, sports results, or physical fitness. But it can also work with things that are harder to quantify, like relationships, quality of life, happiness, or even something like morale. This gets down to the fundamentals of psychology, which is all about understanding how we think and feel. Measuring some of these things may not seem obvious, but the approach allows you to at least have a starting point, gain some knowledge, and evolve.

The nice thing about using analytics is that you will never actually fail. You may reach your desired goal - which, of course, is great. But you may also learn in a quantifiable way what *doesn't* work. That is progress in itself.

For instance, a large casino chain discovered that raising the salary of employees to the average midpoint for that position reduced turnover from 16% to 9%.[5] It would be intuitive to think that going beyond the midpoint would reduce it even further, but the research actually showed that it wasn't the case at all. It ended up costing the company more, but with no statistically significant difference in turnover.

So, did the project fail? Absolutely not! They learned that increasing salary beyond the midpoint was not a motivator to reduce turnover. To reduce it further, they had to try something different. It is sort of like playing the game of "20 questions", where there is an answer, but you have to ask questions until you have enough information to know what the answer is. You can't ask the same question over and over again and expect a different result. You have to learn-and-fail before you can successfully know the answer. Your mother told you as a kid to "learn from your mistakes - don't repeat them." Why not apply this philosophy to HR challenges as well?

FAILURE TO COMMUNICATE

In the movie *Cool Hand Luke*,[6] there is a quote from a scene that Guns N' Roses made famous in their song "Civil War," where the Captain says to Luke:

"What we've got here is failure to communicate." - Strother Martin, as the Captain

In the growing world of data and analytics, data scientists and statisticians tend to struggle to describe what they are seeing in the data to the lay person. Likewise, non-data scientists and non-statisticians tend to struggle to figure out what to measure.

The two sides often have difficulties hearing what the other is trying to say. It's a true "failure to communicate" moment. When thinking about this in terms of analytical versus non-analytical people, it is actually easy to understand the discrepancy. But think about the other scenarios too:

1. Analytical people talking to analytical people: these discussions tend to turn into battles where each person believes their analytical results are stronger.

2. Non-analytical people talking to non-analytical people: similarly, these discussions tend to turn into battles where each person believes their gut feelings are stronger.

It doesn't have to be this way, though. As you learn how to apply the DATA-INSIGHT-ACTION technique to every problem you have, you will begin to ask the right questions and give the right directions.

I'm not suggesting you have to be a data scientist in order to achieve success. *Quantifiably Better* is all about taking what are seemingly difficult things to do and applying this simple approach, so that you can worry about other bigger or more urgent problems to solve. By practicing these steps repeatedly, over time, they just become habit and fundamental to the way you take on any challenge.

DON'T OVERTHINK IT

Actor Anthony Hopkins was once quoted as saying:

"We are dying from overthinking. We are slowly killing ourselves by thinking about everything. Think. Think. Think. You can never trust the human mind anyway. It's a death trap."[7]

Mr. Hopkins is absolutely correct. How many times have you talked yourself out of doing something simply because you began to overthink it and worry about it? Worrying about what *might* happen never is as effective as measuring what *actually* happens.

Using the DATA-INSIGHT-ACTION approach, you will never worry about taking on the risk of something new again. So, if you want to reduce turnover, just follow the process and you will reduce turnover. Then you won't have to worry about it anymore. You know: *one less thing*.

Key Point

Quantifiably Better is all about using the magic formula of DATA-INSIGHT-ACTION to solve problems. Memorize these three simple words.

CHAPTER 2
Understanding Your Data:
The Seven C's

In Chris Gardner's "Start Where You Are," he discusses the importance of taking baby steps, as long as you are moving forward and not worrying about "conquering Rome."[8] It is a walk-before-you-run concept, and this rule definitely applies to understanding your HR data as well.

I have spoken with hundreds of HR leaders who are absolutely terrified about the thought of looking at data on their employees - and I'm not talking about the privacy aspects. They typically claim that the quality of the data in their HR systems is not very good. I usually ask them, "how would you know if you've never looked?" In fact, this was the same question I had when I first delved into the unknown of HR data. But I had learned an important lesson in a previous job where I was in charge of data quality:

Data will NEVER be perfect. It just has to be good enough.

Jack Canfield, author of the *Chicken Soup for The Soul* series, describes the importance of committing yourself to constant and never-ending improvement.[9] I have always felt this was a characteristic worth having. You can always be a little better. But you first have to get to "good enough." So how do you know what "good enough" is, especially when it comes to data?

There are seven ways I have used to measure data quality. This is actually pretty easy to remember, too - you simply need to know the seven C's.

THE SEVEN C'S

1. Certainty

2. Coverage

3. Completeness

4. Consistency

5. Currency

6. Commonality

7. Chance

The seven C's are where you should begin if you are thinking about your data for the first time. In other words, before you can consider how to apply HR analytics, you should understand what you have first. The formulas shared are merely examples of ways to measure each of the seven C's. The idea here is that you go into learning about your data with a game plan. The seven C's provide that initial game plan.

NOTE: there is an eighth "C" related to data, but it is not necessarily part of measuring data quality. The eighth "C" is Consent, and it is important to consider how much you want your employees to know about what you are doing with their data. In many European countries, you are restricted from even looking at the data without first gaining consent from the person. Take this into consideration as you begin your journey, as data privacy, data security, and data governance are all additional things that require attention. But don't let this eighth "C" prevent you from moving forward. Looking at personal data is typically something you can do legally, provided you de-identify or anonymize it initially. Fortunately, in this case, the employees and managers will be able to see the same data you are looking at. Discussion of the eighth "C" could fill a book all by itself, and it will not be discussed in *Quantifiably Better*.

THE FIRST OF THE SEVEN C'S - CERTAINTY

Certainty is simply a word that describes how accurate, truthful, or correct the data is. In most HR cases, the data is simply verified by asking employees whether the information is correct, and then changed by the employee if it is found to be erroneous. So, one way you can measure certainty is to see how many employees make changes when you ask them to verify the information.

$$\text{Certainty} = \frac{\# \text{ of employees who did not make any changes}}{\text{Total } \# \text{ of employees}}$$

This measure of certainty quantifies how many people had perfect data. In other words, if every single employee made no changes, then you would have perfect data. In reality, this is rarely the case. In fact, when you start to think about areas such as Talent Management, where you have the added complexity of managers entering data on employees, it is not possible for the employee to verify the information. You may have to ask the managers, in which case a second measure may be required.

$$\text{Certainty} = \frac{\# \text{ of records tha\ required no changes by managers}}{\text{Total } \# \text{ of employees}}$$

In some cases, you can measure certainty without asking the employee or manager to verify data, because people make mistakes. For example, if you are trying to verify email addresses, you can send a confirmation email to the employee's email on record, and simply determine how many emails are "bounced back" from invalid email addresses.

There isn't a simple guideline to follow on how accurate the data needs to be before it is "good enough." But typically, if you can get to 70% certainty or better, your data is definitely in good shape. In practice, you will find that it is typically in the 90%+ range.

THE SECOND OF THE SEVEN C'S - COVERAGE

Coverage describes how many records actually have the information that you desire. It can be easily measured by understanding how populated a particular element may be.

$$\text{Coverage} = \frac{\# \, of \, employee \, records \, with \, values \, for \, the \, element}{\# \, of \, employees \, tha \; \; should \, have \, values \, for \, the \, element}$$

For example, suppose you are interested in understanding your 401-k coverage. You can simply count the number of employees that are putting money into the 401-k and divide it by the number of employees who are eligible to put money into the 401-k (or you can divide by the total number of employees - just stay consistent with your approaches). Coverage is typically one of the easiest things to measure, and is often one of the best places to start.

In predictive analytics, I often will use a simple 5% rule. If the field is 5% populated, then it has enough data to be of value. This rule can be especially valuable as you introduce new fields to collect, as it can often take time to gain enough coverage for the data to be valuable. For example, suppose you want to know the coverage of self-driven cars owned by your employees. Since self-driven cars are still an emerging trend (at least, as of 2017), it may be years before you have adequate coverage to draw conclusions.

Coverage is also a valuable data measurement when you are considering data acquisition to augment your data. It could be described as measuring the overlap between two sources – that is, how many records from the new source match your existing source.

$$Coverage = \frac{\#\ of\ matching\ records\ from\ acquisition\ dataset}{Total\ \#\ of\ employees}$$

Typically, the higher the measure of coverage, the better.

THE THIRD OF THE SEVEN C'S – COMPLETENESS

Completeness is a measure of whether you have enough data in your total collection of elements to have a comprehensive assessment of the employee.

$$Completeness = \frac{\#\ of\ fields\ you\ have\ populated\ to\ an\ acceptable\ level}{\#\ of\ fields\ you\ have\ (or\ need)}$$

The lack of a completeness measure often serves as a barrier to taking a data-driven step forward. For example, I had a customer once tell me they weren't willing to do anything with HR data analytics until they collected education data on their employees, because otherwise, their data was incomplete.

They should have realized that over 90% of the fields they collected about their employees met the simple rule of being at least 5% filled. In fact, their education data was about 50% filled, which was definitely enough data for effective analysis. I tried to assure them that collecting the additional education data would be a costly and timely exercise, and ultimately, the value the effort provided wouldn't be worth it. They still refused to buckle. They wanted their completeness value to be 100%.

As a result, I knew they were never going to be able to move forward using data to complement their "gut feel" approach.

They were doubters instead of believers that the data they had was going to provide value. They simply could not get past the mental hurdle that suggested all of the data to be fully populated before any value from the data could be obtained.

In other cases, though, it may be important to stop and collect appropriate data before taking a step forward. Imagine you have an employee who is showing frequent absences, and as a result, they begin to show up on possible termination or questionable performance lists. In actuality, the person simply is dealing with a crisis of some kind - and in many cases, the manager is aware, but there is nothing in your HR systems that contain this important data point. This would be an example where the field you need (a flag identifying that a person is going through a personal crisis) is simply not available, thus the data is incomplete. You would need to consider adding a way to collect that field, if it is one that you deem important.

In practice, completeness is used to best understand whether you will be drawing your conclusions from adequate insight. If your overall measure of Completeness is high, then you can feel confident with your conclusions. If it is low, then your conclusions may be incomplete, although still acceptable.

Most importantly, do not think your measure of Completeness needs to be 100% before you can get value out of the data.

THE FOURTH OF THE SEVEN C'S - CONSISTENCY

Consistency is a measure of how stable your data is. To measure this, you need data across different points in time.

$$\text{Consistency} = \frac{\#\ of\ field\ values\ that\ are\ the\ same\ in\ time\ A\ and\ time\ B}{\#\ of\ fields\ evaluated}$$

Consistency is important, since measuring unstable things will only lead to unstable recommendations. Employee Engagement surveys provide good examples of the importance of consistency. If you ask the exact same questions to your employees every so often, the results you get back will be consistent, so you can most likely use the results to compare one time period to another. But if you re-word things, or make attempts to add new things, then you will likely be making decisions based on inconsistent data.

For example, suppose in one Employee Engagement survey, you ask for the employee to fill in their age by selecting from age bands (ex. 20-30, 30-40, 40-50, 50+). In your follow up survey, you change the way you ask, opting for larger bands (20-35, 35-50, 50-65, 65+). The way the data was collected was inconsistent, so you may run into problems in your analytics.

Another example is to look at someone's paycheck. The bi-weekly payment amount may be almost always the same for a salaried employee (or at least within a few cents based on rounding), thus it is very consistent. But an hourly employee may have a fluctuating schedule from pay period to pay period, so their data would be inconsistent.

THE FIFTH OF THE SEVEN C'S - CURRENCY

Currency is the measure of how recent the information in question is .

$$Currency = \frac{\text{\# of employees with data updates since time X}}{Total \text{ \# of employees}}$$

"Time since" can be measured in seconds, minutes, hours, weeks, days, months, years, decades - whatever makes sense for a given field. What is important is that you want to make data-driven decisions based off of recent data.

For example, suppose you are trying to measure employee or candidate sentiment by using their Facebook data. Some of your employees and candidates may post things on a daily basis, while others may only post things on occasion. If you are looking for changes in sentiment, it would only be effective to consider those who post things frequently.

HR examples in which it is common to see currency challenges include areas such as marital status, hours worked, or number of dependents. Even home address is starting to pop as something that is harder to keep current, since so many things are done online through online payment systems, cell phones, and email; employees have no need to update their demographic information like they did many years ago.

Some systems have time stamps where you would know when a specific field was updated, while others may only have a date representing the entire employee record. Take this into consideration as you create your currency metric.

THE SIXTH OF THE SEVEN C'S - COMMONALITY

Commonality is a measure of how unique data is. If you know you have collected data that is truly unique in comparison to your peers' data, then take advantage of that.

$$\text{Commonality} = \frac{\textit{How many of your peers collect this type of data?}}{\textit{How many peers do you have?}}$$

In HR, every company has typically collected information that their peers do not have. But let's think about something like benchmarking. Suppose you find a company that has collected benchmarking data to describe salaries in a way that you have never seen before. This data would be very unique, and therefore more valuable than the data that is offered to everyone else.

Another way to consider commonality is the inverse of coverage. For example, suppose you are hiring for a hard-to-fill position. Your current approach is only yielding 10 potential candidates. You discover a new source that is able to find 100 potential candidates, but it has 6 of the 10 same candidates your original process identified. That means the commonality between the two sources is the overlap, as shown in Figure 2.1.

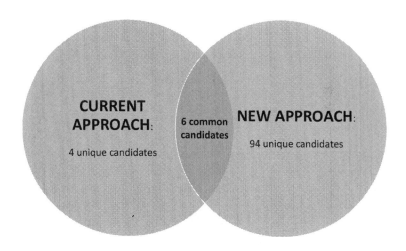

Figure 2.4: Commonality between new and current approaches

When thinking about it this way, each approach has a commonality measure.

$$Commonality = \frac{How\ many\ records\ are\ in\ common\ wit\ \ Source\ A\ and\ Source\ B?}{How\ many\ records\ are\ in\ Source\ A?}$$

$$Commonality = \frac{How\ many\ records\ are\ in\ common\ with\ Source\ A\ and\ Source\ B?}{How\ many\ records\ are\ in\ Source\ B?}$$

In this example, source A has 60% commonality (6 out of 10), while source B has only 6% commonality (6 out of 100). In this case, smaller commonality is better.

In other cases, you may want the commonality to be high in order to confirm your data. For example, suppose you are trying to verify Social Security Numbers (SSNs) in your population to try to identify those that are committing identity fraud. You partner with a third party and find that 95% of your SSNs match up, as shown in Figure 2.2.

Figure 2.5: Commonality with SSNs

You don't really care how unique *their data* is, but you certainly care that 95% is the overlap with *your* data.

THE SEVENTH OF THE SEVEN C'S - CHANCE

Measuring chance is actually a measure of the predictability of the data. While this one may sound the scariest, it is actually one of the best ways to know if the data is "good enough". The reason is pretty simple. Each of the other six C's can be measured for each attribute. Chance can be used to gauge how valuable the data is as a whole. Thankfully, it is pretty easy to measure by using something called a confusion matrix.

	Event happens	Event doesn't happen
You predict an event	You got it right (True positive)	You guessed wrong (False positive)
You predict a non-event	You guessed wrong (False negative)	You got it right (True negative)

Measuring chance isn't too difficult if you use this technique:

$$\text{Chance} = \frac{How\ many\ times\ did\ you\ guess\ right?}{How\ many\ guesses\ did\ you\ make?}$$

If the data is bad, then most likely your predictions will be too. If the data is good enough, your predictions should be pretty good as well.

To get an idea about what a good chance measure might be, consider the effectiveness of credit scores. Banks and lenders use credit scores to "guess" the likelihood of a person paying back the loan. A typical credit score will be correct about 80% of the time, based on setting cutoffs around how much risk they are willing to assume. That is, the true positive + true negative covers 80% of the population.

Considering how dependent the lending system is on credit scores, you can definitely assume that a chance score of 80% must be pretty good. There is no perfect number to use here, though, because that number will vary depending on what you are predicting, as well as cutoff values. Since I am a data scientist and statistician myself, you will be happy to know that in *every case* in which I have measured chance with HR data, the data has always met high predictability measures (>70% correct).

In other words, if you are one of those HR leaders who is worried about going into predictive analytics due to the quality of your data, then maybe you should find something else to worry about. The quality of the data is probably just fine.

CREATING A DATA QUALITY SCORECARD OR DASHBOARD

Having multiple metrics on each of the seven C's is perfectly acceptable. In fact, you will earn points with your C-level by understanding that there are different ways to think about each of these. Now that you can describe the quality of the data in seven different ways (maybe with multiple metrics for each one), you should consider making this something that you look at on a regular basis.

Creating a scorecard or dashboard of some kind is actually a really good way to demonstrate to your C-suite that you have great familiarity of the employee data, and that you are monitoring it to ensure that the data-driven decisions that are being made are based on good data.

There are lots of different ways to create scorecards and dashboards, but I'll share a simple way that can be accomplished with a basic spreadsheet. The goal is to be able to take the seven data quality measures and color code them so that visually, it is easy to spot the problem areas.

To accomplish this, you will need to create some rules that will identify different ranges for each of the seven data quality measures, and then assign a color based on which band the measure falls into. For example, suppose you set up your chance rules as follows:

	Chance > 75%
	Chance is between 65% and 75%
	Chance is below 65%

If your chance measure is 77%, you would make the cell green, suggesting the measure demonstrates a good result.

Supposing you have done this with each of your metrics, your scorecard could look like this:

Certainty	Coverage	Completeness	Consistency	Currency	Commonality	Chance
86%	96%	75%	100%	65%	10%	77%

With a simple glance, one could conclude that the data is pretty high quality overall, since the majority of the cells are green. But maybe the currency needs to be addressed.

It would be very easy to assign weights to determine an overall score as well, so that a single measure could be shared with leaders to prove the quality of the data. For example, maybe you give 3 points for a green, 2 for a yellow, and 1 for a red. Just be consistent in your measure, and you will see how it changes over time. You can probably even assess the cost it would take to move yourself from yellow to green, and the value of doing so. In fact, I encourage you to do so.

You could also make it more aesthetically appealing by using gauges, or some other visualization. If your company has some type of Business Intelligence tool, even better. Find out what your C-suite prefers, and have multiple versions available the first time you present the findings.

Key Points

- Data will NEVER be perfect. It just has to be good enough.

- *Quantifiably Better* suggests seven ways to measure data quality - the seven C's:

    1. Certainty
    2. Coverage
    3. Completeness
    4. Consistency
    5. Currency
    6. Commonality
    7. Chance

- Quiz yourself until you can quickly repeat all 7 from memory. Ask people on your teams to recite them as well. Get to where you are all speaking the same language as quickly as possible.

- *Quantifiably Better* suggests you create a scorecard or dashboard for yourself, and demonstrate to your C-level that you understand the quality of your data.

CHAPTER 3
Manipulating Your Data:
Put Your Stake in the Ground

Many years ago, I was in a situation at work where one of the leaders and I did not see eye to eye on something. He would go and tell his people one thing, and I would go and tell my people something different. He was basing his argument on his gut, and I was basing my argument on information that I had collected from data. I remember specifically the day that he approached me after hearing one of his own employees spout out what I had been saying instead of what he was proposing. Needless to say, he wasn't happy, and he thought I had been weaseling my way into his team's heads, which simply wasn't true.

This leader came right up to me, puffed his chest out at me, and he basically told me to quit going behind his back and telling his people to disagree with him. I had never done such a thing. They just started to look at the same data I had already looked at, and they began to draw the same conclusions.

I remember my wife asking me about it one day, as I would often come home and stew about things he was saying or doing. She asked me why I cared so much about finding a way to work with this guy. What came out of my mouth was something that changed the way I thought about people - I hadn't prepared this statement in advance, but it just came out:

Everybody has a characteristic that I wish I had.

After I said it and thought about it, it was clear to me that this guy had something that I coveted. What was it? Was it power?

Technical skills? The gift of gab? The (unfortunate) gift of being able to B.S. your way out of anything?

I started to ask myself how I could determine if someone had a characteristic that I wish I had in a data-driven way. Was it even possible to measure things like "power" and "the gift of gab"? These terms are nebulous and ripe with opinion. How can they be measured?

Is there a way that I could use the data I have to create the measure? For example, could I measure "power" by looking at the number of direct reports or the amount of budget they manage? Or some combination?

The concept of using the data you have to create something you don't have is what data manipulation is all about.

ATTRIBUTE CREATION

What exactly do I mean by "data manipulation?" I'm not talking about altering the original data. I'm talking about a transformation of the original data into something new and more meaningful. Specifically, it means using one or more fields and one or more rows of data to create a new aggregated attribute of some kind.

There are lots of different types of attributes. They can be quantitative, such as counting how many times something has happened. An example would be the number of absences in the last 6 months. Attributes can also be qualitative. For instance, sentiment analysis could produce a measure indicating whether a person was happy or not.

Predictive analytics can also be thought of as data manipulation. Dictionary.com says that a *predictor* is "a formula for determining additional values or derivatives of a function from the relationship of its given values."[10] In other words, predictive analytics are simply combinations of attributes that attempt to summarize something - say, the likelihood of a specific individual leaving your organization.

Consider this example:

In Marcus Buckingham and Donald O. Clifton's *Now, Discover Your Strengths*,[11] there are 34 different defined themes that are used to describe the type of person you are. These themes, or strengths, each have a name, but are not simply fields that you can pull from your original data. You have to figure out a way to quantify them. A few examples they define include: achiever, analytical, communication, connectedness, developer, fairness, ideation, input, maximizer, responsibility, significance.

What would happen if you had flags in your data that described each one of these? You would have 34 additional flags that would tell you something about each person. Is the individual an achiever that shows great responsibility? Is that someone you might want to put into a leadership program? Think about what could happen if you had these flags in place. You would be able to find common combinations of strengths in your organization, and a smart leader would build their strategy around those strengths. You could also set up mentoring programs based on these strengths.

This is just one example that I got from a book I read. A quick search on Amazon reveals that there are over 180,000 books on leadership alone, so if you are struggling with what to define, I encourage you to read a book, and start thinking about how to measure the characteristics that the book defines.

If you want to make a splash to the C-suite, show statistics about these types of things, instead of the more obvious yawners like employee head counts, which are important, but don't usually yield any kind of excitement. If you can tell your CEO how many people in your company demonstrate the strength of ideation, but they simply aren't in roles where they can leverage that strength, then I guarantee you that they will respond differently than if you simply showed a statistic showing the average salaries between males and females (of course, you may need to do this too for compliance reasons).

Showing something they haven't seen or thought of before is definitely the way to the coveted proverbial "seat at the table." It also brings us back to an earlier point that introducing new knowledge is the way to transform behavior. Take what former Netscape CEO Jim Barksdale said: "If we have data, let's look at data. If all we have are opinions, let's go with mine."[12] He said this in response to being asked how HR leaders can get more attention in the boardroom. He basically said that for HR people to get the required attention, they have to lead with data. Not with opinion alone.

TAKE YOUR DATA KNOWLEDGE TO THE NEXT LEVEL

While there are definitely times when simple IF-this-THEN-that mentality can be easily applied to raw data, in most cases, it is going to take a programmer of some kind to help with data manipulation.

While this could be an opportunity to learn a new skill, it might make more sense to hire someone or partner up with someone who already has these skills. If you can describe what you want, especially by talking through real data examples, someone can code your idea into reality. Manipulating data is much more of an art than a science, and it requires knowledge about the data. Who better to have that knowledge than you?

Knowledge is power. Just remember that facts are facts and cannot be argued. If you come up with a way to measure someone's "fairness" or "ideation" capabilities, it will become the new fact. I refer to this as putting your "stake in the ground" when defining something that is not so obvious. Keep in mind that you are going to have to correlate these new attributes to something meaningful. In other words, if you define ideation at the employee level, you should be prepared to show how it affects productivity or the bottom line.

ANOTHER DETAILED EXAMPLE

In John D. Moyer's excellent book *Personal Intelligence*, he describes the components of what makes up one's "personal intelligence."[13] Part of this includes identifying information about personality, and he breaks this out into two sub-components:

- Reading personality from faces

- Knowing how to use introspection

Without going into great detail, let's think about how you could use data manipulation to create attributes for these two items. What is the first thing you think of when you read the phrase "reading personality from faces"? You probably think of some basic emotions: happy, sad, angry, tired, or crazy, for instance.

It is possible to use facial recognition software to take images of people and define these simple emotions. Maybe that is enough to help you get started with this first item. Even using the most basic of emotions, you could potentially quantify them on each of your employees, simply by evaluating pictures of them, especially at different points in time or during the day.

Next, Moyer describes the importance of "knowing how to use introspection," which is all about how you use your own mental and emotional processes to identify information about personality. This can be accomplished by doing a peer review. Ask the employee's manager and peers if they think the employee is described by a list of these emotions, and maybe leave an area where they can add their own comments.

In doing this simple exercise, you will end up with one of two scenarios:

- The facial recognition software and survey results match

- The facial recognition software and survey results do not match

The first scenario probably makes you feel pretty good. You probably feel pretty confident that you described the employee's personality pretty well.

But what about that second scenario? For example, if the images suggest the person is a happy and crazy person, but the survey suggests the person is sad and angry, then you might feel like you don't have good quality data. But keep in mind that these are just attributes that you are creating.

You don't have to know for certain if there is going to be great *value* in everything you create right out of the gate.

The bottom line is that you now have up to 10 new ways to measure people:

Facial Recognition	Survey Results	New attribute
Happy	Happy	Truly Happy
Happy	Not Happy	Possibly Happy
Sad	Sad	Truly Sad
Sad	Not Sad	Possibly Sad
Angry	Angry	Truly Angry
Angry	Not Angry	Possibly Angry
Tired	Tired	Truly Tired
Tired	Not Tired	Possibly Tired
Crazy	Crazy	Truly Crazy
Crazy	Not Crazy	Possibly Crazy

This is what "data manipulation" is all about: creating new and innovative ways to describe something. You are simply leveraging the data from its original state into a more useful state that you can reuse over and over again. You aren't editing the original data (which would be a totally different type of data manipulation), but adding to it.

THE SHOCKINGLY COMPLEX EXAMPLE OF TENURE

If you are an HR leader, you likely have access to both your current and former employees' data records. Suppose you simply want to measure the tenure of both. In the case of current employees, you can simply create an attribute that counts the number of months or years the person has been employed. This is easily done by subtracting the original date of hire from today's date.

But what about the former employees? You can probably do this pretty easily too, by subtracting their original date of hire from their date of termination. By doing so, you now would know both the tenure of your current employees, as well as your former employees.

This seems rather straightforward, but the section title suggests this may not be as simple as it sounds. For example, what if the employee has left and come back - is his tenure based on the original hire date or his most recent hire date?

What if the data has some sort of weird anomaly, where the person appears to have been employed for 115 years (because the system recorded the person started in 1901 instead of 2001)?

Examples like these are very common - and in general, unless you are trying to create a data business, it is not going to matter how you decide to handle the data anomalies.

What is critical though is that whatever you do, you do it *consistently*, so that you are applying the same logic to everybody. Consistent rules will keep the data clean, repeatable, and non-controversial.

This is where data quality comes into play once again. You can simply take each of the attributes you create, and run them through the seven C's. Not only will this help you quantify the quality of your new data, but it will help you gain a larger understanding of the data and what it represents, in general.

Key Points

- Everybody has good characteristics. Find and measure them.

- Data manipulation is all about creating things that are not obvious. Create ways to measure what you thought could not be measured.

- Be consistent when applying rules when doing data manipulation. Whatever you create will become the new truth and fact.

CHAPTER 4
Monitoring Your Data:
Follow Everything

One of the most difficult things I see occurring with HR leaders who begin to dabble with analytics is that the INSIGHT does not match up with their hunch. Say the following out loud:

I am not always right with my assumptions.

This is a difficult statement to make. It instantly suggests that you are flawed in some way. Maybe after saying this, you feel like you are not worthy of the position you are in. Don't worry - you are no different than any other HR or business leader out there. They also have made assumptions about data with similar results. They have also had to figure out how to save face or grow tougher skin.

This is where the value of INSIGHT begins to really take shape. As you have learned so far, facts are facts and cannot be debated. When you have knowledge about the data, you can speak to others with more confidence, as you likely have real facts to fall back on, and not just guesses or feelings.

Hopefully, you not only have a dashboard of INSIGHT about the quality of the data, but also a dashboard of INSIGHT on the new data attributes that you created. These new insights are starting to take shape, and you may begin to see areas where your company may be strong or weak.

MANAGING ANALYSIS PARALYSIS

Gertrude Stein was once quoted as saying, "Everybody gets so much information all day long that they lose their common sense."[14] This was written in 1946, but it applies just as much today as it did back then. I can only imagine what Gertrude Stein would be thinking in this day and age of constant data and information bombardment.

When you have a couple of charts to share in a presentation, it is definitely consumable by the audience. But if you try to capture and analyze all of the new data you acquire each day, you might experience what is known as "analysis paralysis."

Simply put, "analysis paralysis" occurs when you have so many results to consider that you don't really know where to begin. This is not an envious place to be. In one of my roles, I was monitoring over 100,000 attributes every day. I wasn't looking at charts and distributions of every attribute every day, as this would have been impossible. But I did look for outliers or unusual behavior by simply comparing data from the prior day/week/month to the current picture.

One way to monitor lots of data without ever touching it is to set up control charts for each that are automatically published to you, or perhaps generated on the fly through Business Intelligence software. You will want to set up upper and lower control limits based on means and standard deviations - these can easily be generated, so this is not an odious task.

If the current data climbs over or under one of these control limits, it alerts you to take a look. You can have the system send you an automated email or notification to your cell phone that an attribute is outside of the norm and requires attention. Keep in mind that this is not just for the raw data, but also for your newly-created attributes. You can literally monitor everything this same way.

Most academic material will suggest you set your upper and lower control limits at three standard deviations away from the average. About 99.7% of the variation happens within 3 standard deviations of the mean. In other words, if you used a threshold of three standard deviations as your limits, you would only trigger about 0.3% notifications. That is, 0.3 notifications per 100 attributes.

Control Limit = Average of attribute value $\pm$ 3 standard deviations

If you are monitoring thousands of attributes, you may be getting more notifications per evaluation than you can handle. To adjust for this, simply increase the threshold by selecting a higher number of standard deviations. In the role where I was monitoring 100,000 attributes, I used six standard deviations away from the norm, which reduced my notifications to about 5 per month, or 0.005%. You will likely have to experiment with this a little bit to figure out what baseline works best for you. I would target no more than 5-9 attributes per month to avoid analysis paralysis.

WHEN DATA CROSSES A CONTROL LIMIT

Suppose that you are monitoring the monthly turnover of your company. The average monthly turnover is 2%, and the standard deviation is 0.25%:

2% $\pm$ (3 * 0.25%)

In other words, you don't want to really worry about turnover unless your turnover is less than

2% - (3 * 0.25%) = 1.25%

or if your turnover is greater than

$$2\% + (3 * 0.25\%) = 2.75\%$$

Otherwise, while it may be interesting to know the latest figures, it should not be triggering your attention. Suppose that one month, your turnover is at 3%. Is this reason for alarm? Perhaps. This is when you want to pull up your control chart to see if this is expected. There are a couple of likely scenarios.

Scenario 1: The turnover rate is very abnormal. Figure 4.1 shows what this scenario might look like.

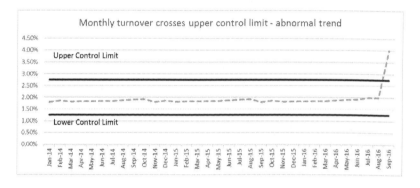

Figure 4.1: Monthly turnover, abnormal trend

You can see that historically the turnover rate has stayed within the lower control limit (label LCL) and upper control limit (label UCL). Suddenly, in September 2016, the turnover rate has spiked. So, is it reason for alarm? Maybe you just had a large reduction in force, or perhaps a re-org took place (re-org's cause a statistically significant increase in turnover). In either of these cases, you could explain the unusual activity. But what if there wasn't an obvious cause?

Maybe one of your key leaders retired, and his retirement persuaded others to follow. Maybe one of your key leaders left for another role, and the morale of his department is now in danger. You could start to see if there is a causal relationship with any of your attributes. In other words, find out which attributes are correlated with turnover, and then look at the control chart for that attribute. See if you see the same behavior. If you do, maybe you found the cause, or at least a correlation.

For example, suppose you created your 10 "emotion" attributes as defined in the last chapter, and you notice a very similar (but inverted) trend in your TRULY HAPPY attribute. Figure 4.2 shows what this might look like.

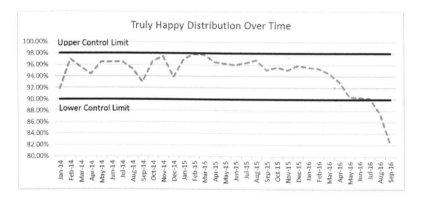

Figure 4.2: Truly happy distribution over time

You can see that as early as 2015, the distribution of TRULY HAPPY started to trend down, but it really dropped sharply in the last 2 months, below the lower control limit. In other words, TRULY HAPPY could have been a leading indicator to suggest that turnover was going to be a problem.

Now imagine that you are going in to see the CEO to share the bad news that turnover is up. When she asks why, you are equipped with data. Your answer could be that "our employees have shown problems with being happy, especially over the last two months". You then have a nice open discussion about how the departure of a key product manager caused others in his department to experience a change in their emotional status, eventually causing turnover to occur.

In looking at the data of TRULY HAPPY, you might even point out that it appears that TRULY HAPPY employees started to decline back in early 2015, which coincided with the hiring of a new Chief Marketing Officer. Could it be that his hiring actually influenced the product manager to leave? You aren't suggesting the hiring of the CMO was bad, but you are simply able to potentially tie two events together whose downstream impact could cost the company millions. Let the CEO figure out that it was a bad hire or a bad fit. Hopefully, you can sense how this discussion is a very different discussion, since it is much more based on fact than gut feel.

I can assure you that the CEO will listen to you next time you point out that you are seeing something in the data that is concerning to you, especially if it ties back to something that is important to her, such as income, cost to hire, a reduction in sales, or a declining net promoter score in the market place. The bottom line is that by having the data at your fingertips, the conversation was about the data. You weren't surprised by any of her questions, and you gained credibility.

Scenario 2: The turnover rate has been trending that way for some time. Crossing the upper control limit is normal and expected. It is simply time to reset the trigger mechanism. Figure 4.3 on the facing page shows what this scenario might look like.

Beginning in January 2015, the turnover rate has been on a general upward slope. Where you have typically told the CEO that the average monthly turnover was 2%, you may need to revise her expectations. The cause of the upward trend would be investigated the same way as it was in Scenario 1. It could be due to key people leaving, a badly trending TRULY HAPPY attribute, or some other cause. Again though, the conversation you have with the CEO is different than if your hunch was based on gut feeling alone.

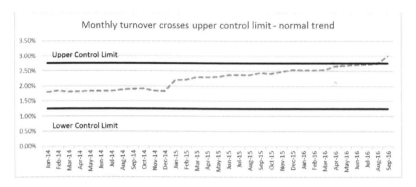

Figure 4.3: Monthly turnover, normal trend

You point out that the turnover rate crossed the upper control limit, and you hopefully share data that backs up the cause. But in this case, you tell the CEO that this was expected. As a result, you will be changing the control limits based on the new information. You point out that to get it back to where it was, you could create a retention strategy to put in place. If you have done your part with predictive analytics, hopefully you can point out that you know which specific employees are most likely to leave next, and that your retention program will target these employees and their managers only, keeping costs down.

Again, the conversation is about the data. When you are armed with good data, you can come in with a plan of attack and a positive message, even when the message isn't necessarily good news. The CEO will not only start to rely on you for guidance, but you may even be given a larger budget (especially after you show her that reduced turnover increases stock price in another chart you have created).

TURNING DATA INTO SMART DATA

As you continue to experiment with presenting your data in different ways, you will likely feel some of the phenomenon of "analysis paralysis." This is normal. The secret to being successful with HR analytics is not to present everything you are measuring. It is to present the things that tie to important business outcomes.

If the CEO wants to know the salary distribution of males to females for different job levels, make sure that is what you present. But also, add in the things that you believe could be causing them to be different. Simple correlations are great starting points from which to figure out causal relationships. Remember, though, that correlation does not always equal causation. For example, it is pretty easy to prove that tenure is correlated with turnover. People who stay a long time are likely to continue to stay. But it isn't the cause. You would need to tap into your other attributes to try to find a cause.

People who know me hear me say things like "measure a million things, but only show the top 3." This is a really important principle to avoid "analysis paralysis".

THE HR GPS SYSTEM

I have mentioned the many discussions I have had with HR leaders who insist that their data is of poor quality, but have never looked at it. Much like when using a GPS system, in order to understand where you want to take your company, you need to understand where you are first.

Imagine how poorly your GPS system would perform if it only knew the destination and not the starting point. Are you having those types of conversations with your C-suite, managers, and employees? Credibility always is stronger when you have a starting metric.

Wouldn't it be better to have a data-driven picture of each employee, manager, department, job function, etc.? You would be able to quickly identify the needs of each one of these with a simple click. Suddenly, instead of having broad programs where you treat everyone the same, you can have personalized programs, driven by data, with known and expected results.

For example, suppose you decide to look at which jobs are receiving the highest pay increases year over year. You find that your business systems analysts are showing an upward change in compensation on average of 8.2% year over year, which is significantly higher than the 2.6% change in compensation across other roles in the whole company.

You begin to dig into the data a little bit, and you see that there is one manager in particular who is giving 10-15% raises annually. You look into the talent reviews for those employees, but you find no comments from this manager at all. You look at comments from other managers of business systems analysts, and you see that their average increases are also higher than the normal employee in the company, but nothing like the increases from this one manager.

One scenario might involve you deciding that it would be beneficial to tell ALL managers of systems analysts how compensation reviews should take place and what is expected. This is an expensive ordeal, as you have to order training supplies, bring each of them into training sessions, and pull them away from their day-to-day work, which reduces productivity – even though the vast of managers don't really need it.

The other scenario is more personalized. You meet one-on-one with this particular manager, and you provide some simple guidance as to how compensation reviews should take place and what is expected. The cost savings in the personalized program is substantial.

Maybe this scenario is a little far-fetched to imagine, especially if, for instance, you compensate based on a distinct distribution of overall ratings. For example: 5% of employees receive outstanding ratings, 25% receive above average ratings, 60% receive average ratings, and 10% receive needs improvement ratings. Within each band, the range of increase can only go so high.

Have you ever evaluated your "bell curve" by manager? Nobody wants to be the manager that has no high performing people, so managers always tend to put at least one of their employees in the above average tiers.

There are certainly more realistic scenarios you can think of: studying turnover by manager, succession management by department, or TRULY HAPPY by employee. In any scenario, the INSIGHT you gain will allow you to take decisive ACTION.

DATA WITHOUT INSIGHT

Science fiction writer Daniel Keys Moran has been quoted as saying "You can have data without information, but you cannot have information without data."[15] Do you know what information without data is? It is a hunch or a guess.

DATA without INSIGHT is worthless. It is the equivalent of having all of the ingredients to bake a cake, but no recipe. You can guess how much of each ingredient you might need, but in the end, the cake will most likely not be very good (if it is a cake at all).

Remember when you were learning how to drive a car? You passed the initial test to get your driver's permit, so you only had a limited amount of DATA that was converted into INSIGHT. But you never had any practical use for the INSIGHT until you got behind the wheel. What I am suggesting is that it is time to get in your HR car, set up the HR GPS system, and figure out where you are. Then monitor yourself like crazy to ensure you are going where you want to go.

Key Points

- You are not always going to be right with your assumptions.

- Setting up control limits on all of your elements and attributes is a great way to get in front of the data. You will become the subject matter expert of your employee data, which is what you are expected to be anyway.

- You can only figure out how to get to your destination if you know where you are starting from. Let data be the supplier of your starting point.

- Data without insight is worthless. You have data in your possession. Make it useful.

CHAPTER 5
Preparing For Action:
The Data and Analytics Maturity Model

I have three daughters. As they were growing up, the technology around them was too. My oldest was a VHS kid, and she watched Disney movies over and over again on tapes that would lose quality over time. My middle daughter was a DVD kid, and she was able to not only watch Disney movies over and over again, she was able to watch individual scenes with a simple click back to the DVD Menu. There are certain songs from some of those movies that haunt me to this day due to excessive repetition. I would bet many of you share my experience.

My youngest, though, has been raised on smartphones and tablets. She barely has any concept of needing a special physical piece of media, or special equipment to play that media. She doesn't even require a separate TV screen to watch the display that is generated from the special equipment - in her mind, she can just stream whatever she wants to watch on whatever device she has handy. The "screen" is always in her hands. It is truly a fascinating transition that has taken place in a relatively short period of time.

One of the movies that my youngest (and the rest of the family) enjoys is "The Croods." In one scene, the family father, named Grug, is listening to a story from a young boy, named Guy, who is not part of the family. Grug doesn't trust Guy. Grug has always been in charge, and suddenly, Guy is sharing an alternative way of seeing the world that is making Grug uncomfortable. The scene goes like this:[16]

Guy: Once upon a time, there was a beautiful tiger. She lived in a cave with the rest of her family. Her father and mother told her: "You may go anywhere you want, but never go near the cliff, for you could fall."

Grug (sarcastically, interrupting Guy's final words): And die. Good story.

Guy: But when no one was looking, she'd go near the cliff, for the closer she came to the edge, the more could she hear, the more could she see, the more she could feel. Finally, she stood at the very edge. She saw a light. She leaned out to touch it... and she slipped.

Grug (sarcastically again): And she fell.

Guy (dramatically): And she flew.

I love this quote. I love the mental image this creates when I think about HR leaders who are just starting to get to the point where they have great new INSIGHT about their employees. You have an opportunity to *fly*, when everyone else is simply staying away from the edge of the cliff.

The scene gets even better, and the children, Thunk and Eep, begin to ask questions as well:

Thunk: Where did she fly?

Guy: Tomorrow.

Eep: Tomorrow?

Guy: A place with more suns in the sky than you can count.

Thunk: It would be so bright!

Guy: A place not like today, or yesterday. A place where things are better.

Grug (angrily): Tomorrow isn't a place. It's-it's-it... Ugh! You can't see it!

Guy: Oh, yes, yes, it is. I've seen it. That's where I'm going.

The tiger flew to tomorrow. She wasn't flying backwards or circling around. She flew forward and got to the place where something was more amazing than anything she had ever seen. Guy claims to have seen it too (note the transition from talking about the tiger to himself in the last phrase). He was clearly impressed, to the point of deciding that "tomorrow" is the only place worth going to.

As you begin to understand your employees with actual DATA and INSIGHT, it will give you an incredible opportunity to modernize your approaches to dealing with your employees. My hope for you is that eventually you won't think of DATA-INSIGHT-ACTION as three separate things, but a single consolidated factory that you use to solve problems.

Don't be a Grug. Go and fly to tomorrow. And take others with you.

LEARNING THE ROPES

When you onboard a new employee, one of the best things to do is have them interview leaders that their role will impact. They will learn that there are important details in their job that they may not have been aware of prior to starting the role. This is often referred to as "learning the ropes."

For many HR leaders, moving toward a data-driven approach may feel a little bit like starting their career over in certain regards. Similar to a new employee, it definitely makes sense to talk with leaders about what you are about to do to ensure that you are on the right path. While you are learning about data, they live and die by data every day.

Finding out how different leaders measure their own success is critical to getting their support for what you are doing. In other words, while reducing turnover may be important for you, the Chief Operating Officer may spend his days being evaluated on website metrics, or the time it takes to onboard a new customer. You need to find a way to tie the metrics that are important to him to the metrics that you have to offer.

For example, suppose you have created your TRULY HAPPY attribute discussed in Chapter 3. If you can show that the website metrics for a certain function are stronger in the part of the organization where more TRULY HAPPY employees reside, then you have the data to support the need to make other parts of the organization TRULY HAPPY. That might include suggesting organizational changes or putting certain managers through some type of training.

Similarly, the Chief Marketing Officer might be trying to show the effectiveness of their advertising spending. If you can show that the response rates are higher on the ads that were generated by the teams that have more TRULY HAPPY employees, then suddenly your metrics are going to be evaluated differently.

You may even begin to capture TRULY HAPPY during the recruiting and interview process, so that you bring on the most TRULY HAPPY employees you can. You will definitely have the full support of your leaders, as they will recognize that TRULY HAPPY employees are fulfilling their needs better.

How you go about exposing your analytics and tying those analytics to the business is going to take some time. It will take discipline on your part, because you are likely going to want to share your findings as soon as you have them. But until you can tie those results to what is important to others, you will be your own cheerleader. It is way more fun when everyone wants what you have to offer.

SUCCESS LEAVES CLUES

In motivational speaker Tony Robbins' book *Unlimited Power*, he makes the following statement:

"Long ago, I realized that success leaves clues, and that people who produce outstanding results do specific things to create those results."[17]

When you begin to go down the path of having a data-driven HR department, you actually prove this quote to be true. Why? You aren't working solely from your gut anymore - instead you have INSIGHT that backs up every step.

There is a key word in this sentence, though, that you may have overlooked: it is the word *do*. The quote doesn't say that people who produce outstanding results generate amazing charts and visualizations. It says that these people *do something* to create great results.

In 1956, cognitive psychologist George A. Miller produced a paper that is frequently referenced amongst psychologists called "The Magical Number Seven, Plus or Minus Two: Some Limits on Our Capacity for Processing Information."[18] The theory is that the brain can only process so much stimulation at any instant point in time: 5 to 9 things, to be precise.

Based on this theory, if a manager is trying to manually keep up with more than 5 to 9 attributes on his employees at a given point in time, he would benefit by having guidance provided to him. For example, typical good predictive analytics algorithms contain 30+ attributes, which is why they can be so valuable in your journey. The human brain simply cannot comprehend this many details simultaneously. Similarly, if the right action requires a complex calculation of 30+ clues, trying to do this instantaneously in your mind is almost impossible.

How you discover the clues is another story. If you have generated a group of attributes with the data manipulation step, then you will be ahead of the curve. You will start to be able to tie the opinionated ways to measure things (like engagement, culture, and high potentials) to the non-opinionated ways to measure things (like sales, growth, or productivity).

In Malcolm Gladwell's outstanding book *Outliers: The Story of Success*, he discusses how it takes 10,000 hours to become an expert at something.[19] That is the equivalent of 5 years' worth of work - 40 hours a week for 5 straight years. You cannot and should not expect to be perfect in practicing the discovery of clues immediately.

And you should not be afraid to share this point with the business. Tell the leadership team where you are in your journey, and that your next steps are to start to ACT on all of the INSIGHT that you have found. They may ask questions about the specific actions you are going to take, and your response should be that you do not know yet. Make sure you include the word *yet*. Emphasize it.

You may even persuade your leadership team to hire a data and analytics person to help you. They might even fund it if they are seeing the benefit.

DAILY CHANGE FOR SUCCESS

I hope that by reading this chapter, you are beginning to understand the challenge that lies before you. You are trying to change human behavior, which is not going to be easy or quick. A client of mine told me that changing the culture of an organization is not something you can do with a single decision. It is something that occurs slowly, much like a shift in the economy. Sometimes a single event can move the needle a little faster than others, but typically, a series of events is required for sustaining change.

But that change won't likely get kicked off unless you choose to *do* something that is different. It will not happen magically, but instead starts with the first of many changes that will be applied daily. I'm not only talking about personal change here - I'm talking about influencing others to make daily changes as well.

Famous motivational speaker and author Jim Rohn said that "success is nothing more than a few simple disciplines, practiced every day."[20] In my personal experience, when I've had a large task involving change ahead of me, I have always told my own employees that the only way to eat an elephant is to take a bite. We celebrated after every bite. Measuring progress is an incredibly motivating experience of accomplishment.

To become intimately familiar with a data-driven approach, you have to start somewhere. Throughout the first four chapters of this book, I have suggested three important concepts:

1. Create REPORTS on your data quality by applying the seven C's

2. MANIPULATE the original data to reveal new insights that you did not have

3. MONITOR all of the original data and the attributes you have created on a regular basis, so that when someone asks a question, you either know the answer, or you know where to get it

Now, we look at the next step.

4. PREPARE for action by figuring out what is most important to your business' leaders and customers

The combination of these concepts are what I call The Data and Insight Maturity Model, and it demonstrates the relationship between your familiarity with the data and your readiness for data-driven action. Figure 5.1 illustrates this relationship.

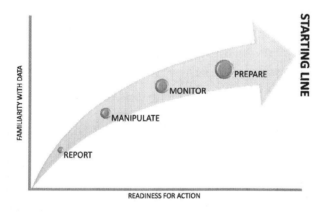

Figure 5.1: The Data and Insight Maturity Model

Theoretically, you should not even consider taking any kind of action until you have spent time in each of the four steps above. In other words, if you run some initial REPORTS on your data, but haven't gone through the MANIPULATE / MONITOR / PREPARE steps, you won't be as prepared as someone who has carried out all of these steps.

The point of this model is simple: if you don't have enough familiarity with the data, then you are simply using your gut and instincts to decide what will happen next.

Use the Data and Insight Maturity Model to describe your strategy and approach to leadership. They will appreciate you having a plan, even though it may be a little fuzzy at first.

If you do all of these things, your familiarity with your employees is going to take a significant step forward. Not only that, your familiarity with the business is also going to take a significant step forward. You won't be alone in understanding the business, but you may be the lone wolf in understanding your employees and how they relate to a successful business.

As you promote the learnings that you are gaining each step of the way, the business leaders will begin to turn to you as a source of INSIGHT, which is exactly the goal of becoming data-driven. You are going to gain significant importance in the eyes of the leadership team. Do not take this for granted, because their expectations are going to increase as well, which is why it is so important to accept where you are first and prepare for the next steps.

Key Points

- Find out what your business leaders measure before you take any action. You need to tie your upcoming actions to their measures to be most effective.

- Change doesn't happen overnight. You have to eat the elephant one bite at a time.

- Share the Data and Insight Maturity Model when talking with leaders about your strategy to become data-driven.

CHAPTER 6
Purpose-Driven Analytics:
Understanding Motivators

I have been managing employees for over 20 years. The first time was the hardest, as there were lots of unknowns. I moved into the role simply because my boss had decided to resign, and I was "next up." I hadn't received any formal training. I was expected to just keep doing what my predecessor was doing.

For managing the actual work, it was easy to pick up where she left off. There was a nice backlog of tasks that needed to be done, so I just assigned out the work using this list. But I had no idea how to plan for the future. I had no strategic plan on how I would manage my employees. I had no idea how difficult it would be to handle different types of situations. I was mostly unprepared.

Thankfully, my prior boss was a good one. I was lucky in seeing a reasonably good model of how to manage people. She had slowly been informally training me to be her successor, even though she may have not even known it. I started to think about three things: (1) the things she did that I liked, (2) the things she did that didn't make sense to me, but others liked, and (3) the things that didn't make sense to any of us. This led me to my first real decision point on what kind of manager I wanted to be.

I wanted to be a manager that did things that my employees wanted. I realized I was going to have to personalize my approach so that I was meeting each of their needs, and avoid the things that would cause friction. And those things would be different for each employee. It wasn't going to be about me.

For me, it meant that I wouldn't be putting into play any "programs" where everyone was treated the exact same way as their neighbor. This was pretty gutsy and counterintuitive to every HR person I spoke with, because their responsibility at that time ended with the creation of "programs" . It was up to the managers and the employees themselves to take the next steps as they saw fit.

Back then, the internet was just getting started, so there wasn't such easy access to information like there is today. I relied on books that described best practices, and I spoke with other managers about how to deal with different situations. I was shocked at how bad people were at understanding what employees really wanted. I wanted to be different. Stephen Graves said that "the desire to be above average runs in all of humanity."[21] But I didn't just want to be above average. I wanted to be the best.

The company I worked for at the time was never on any kind of "best places to work" lists, and one day I asked my boss whether getting onto one of those lists was a goal for the company. His response shook me to the core: "Steve, that isn't realistic." I felt like I had been punched in the gut. I wanted to find out what those good companies were doing and try to duplicate it. Why was that unrealistic?

I couldn't understand how someone could be considered a leader and have no aspirations to make their department or company a "best place to work." In four words, he told me that he didn't care about me or any of his other direct reports, and if that was his attitude, it was likely that he was surrounded by people who also didn't care about me.

I'd be lying if I said it was only those four words. There were additional data points that led me to this final conclusion, including a history of only promoting males, not approving training opportunities, and even eliminating vacations. In my opinion, he wasn't a bad supervisor. But he was a crummy leader, certainly not someone you try to emulate when you are in the midst of career growth. I immediately became what is commonly called a "disengaged" employee. I didn't stop being productive. I just stopped caring. As a result, the quality of my work took an expected hit.

EMPLOYEE ENGAGEMENT AND TURNOVER

It doesn't take a rocket scientist to figure out that the workplace has similar issues today. A quick visit to Gallup.com reveals that only 33% of employees are "engaged." This is roughly the same as it has been for the last 15 years.[22] If you think about that statistic and trend, it means that despite huge amounts of money being spent on improving engagement, it hasn't resulted in any substantial improvement. It means that managers and organizations are just as dysfunctional now as they were 15 or 20 years ago.

Read what Victor Lipman writes:

"If 60% to 70% of employees are working at less than full capacity, an awful lot of you in management are dealing with motivation problems. It also means there's a huge opportunity: an opportunity to better engage employees and improve productivity for your department and organization. To use simple numbers, if you manage 10 employees and six of them are to some extent disengaged, and you can reach on average two of them to better engage and motivate them, those are immediately very significant productivity gains you'll achieve."[23]

This is shocking to me. It is suggesting that a good manager can reach on average two out of ten employees to better engage and motivate them, assuming the three or four who are already "engaged" will remain that way. At best, that means that four out of ten employees are going to remain disengaged no matter what you try or do. Hold that thought for a moment.

In a 2016 survey conducted at tens of thousands of organizations to determine actual turnover rates, the results showed that the annual average turnover rate was 17.8%.[24] The Bureau of Labor Statistics suggests that number was even higher, at 23.6%.[25] For argument's sake, let's meet in the middle and say it is 20%. That means that two out of ten employees are walking out the door every year.

Let's think about this visually. Assume a manager has 10 employees. 4 out of 10 are "disengaged", two are "reached" (per Litman), and 4 are "engaged". We'll call this Scenario Ground Zero.

Scenario Ground Zero:

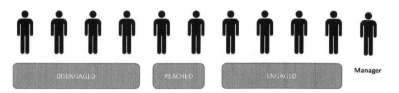

Over the next year, two of those ten are going to leave (marked with an "X.") Organizations *hope* that the following scenario occurs (Scenario 1):

Scenario 1:

In Scenario 1, the number of "disengaged" employees went from four to two. That is potentially a good thing.

If on average 60% of employees are "disengaged", then you have to assume that 60% of the new employees will also be "disengaged". For argument's sake, let's say one of the two ends up "disengaged", and the other is either "reached" or "engaged". This would seem to paint an improved scenario - Scenario 1A – where only 3 out of the 10 employees are "disengaged":

Scenario 1A:

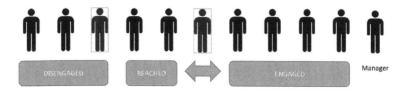

But since trends show that the percentage of employees that are "engaged" has been stuck for 15 years, then it actually suggests that someone from the "reached" or "engaged" group is actually highly likely to shift into the "disengaged" group, leaving you right back where you started: Scenario Ground Zero.

Here is another option - what organizations *hope doesn't* happen (Scenario 2):

Scenario 2:

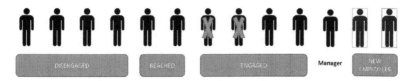

In Scenario 2, the organization lost two of their "engaged" employees. I would argue that this is a more likely scenario. Why? Because "engaged" employees are the most attractive to recruiters. They are productive, and they are typically performing at higher levels.

Using the same logic, you have to assume that at best, only one of the two new employees is going to be "engaged" (Scenario 2A):

Scenario 2A:

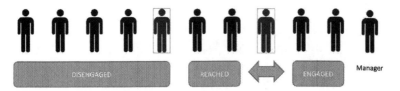

Scenario 2A paints a scary picture, as half of the team is now "disengaged". Again, though, since the trends show that the percent of employees that are "engaged" has been stuck for 15 years, then it actually suggests that someone from the "reached" or "disengaged" group is actually highly likely to shift into the "engaged" group, leaving you right back where you started once again: Scenario Ground Zero.

Because of the stagnancy of the trends, the most likely scenario is one in which you lose one "disengaged" employee and one "reached" or "engaged" employee, and replace them with one of each as well. In other words, nothing really changes too much. Things just stay at Scenario Ground Zero.

But I want you to think about one additional scenario – Scenario 3:

Scenario 3:

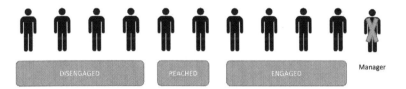

It is important to think about this very common scenario. I never classified the manager into any of the groups in scenarios 1 or 2. But you have to assume that 6 out of 10 managers are "disengaged" or "reached" as well.

The manager is often the person who is pulled out of the group. Similar to the discussion about losing "engaged" employees to competitors, good managers who are "engaged" are highly attractive candidates. But it isn't only voluntary turnover one has to worry about. It could simply be a promotion of some kind into a different part of the organization.

No matter the cause, it still leaves a scenario where either a new manager is promoted from within the team or organization (which can cause "fairness" challenges for the new manager), or the new manager is hired from the outside (which can cause friction with the existing staff, since they felt they were not considered for promotion).

One of my own observations is that far too often, employees who are excellent individual contributors are put into leadership positions for which they are not qualified. They aren't strategic thinkers - they are simply excellent executors.

People like this tend to be good supervisors, and we absolutely need people like that to move our visions forward.

But for leadership, something else is needed. You need someone who can motivate others to achieve something greater. Not only does that person need to paint a futuristic picture of "flying to tomorrow", but they also have to manage to the individual needs of each employee in a very personal way. If a person you want to promote to a leadership position is not qualified to have the capability to personalize how they lead employees, then find someone else - no matter how productive they are.

EMPLOYEE MOTIVATORS

Did I lose you with all of those scenarios? Welcome to the brain of an INTJ (my Myers-Briggs psychological profile, which stands for introversion, intuition, thinking, judgment). Let me simplify.

I think a good manager reaches ten out of ten every day. Anything less is failure in my eyes. It just takes a little DATA and INSIGHT to figure out what a person's motivators really are. If I am able to give each employee what they need when they need it, then their engagement levels rise, and they become happy and highly productive employees. Oh, and turnover goes down, which helps long term business goals be more easily reached.

How do I know this? In my 20+ years of managing people, I have never had a single employee leave for voluntary reasons (minus one employee who decided to go back to school to get her Ph.D., which I fully supported and suggested). I'm a sample of one manager, but I've had 30+ direct reports in those 20+ years. 30+ employees may not sound like a big number, but since none of them ever left, it makes intuitive sense why that number is low. I did it by focusing on what motivated each employee, and then I used those motivators to accomplish our goals.

A search on Google for "employee motivators" returns over 440,000 results. As you begin to look through these various sites and documents, you start to see that there is not going to be any single way to define the things that motivate people. But you will see some common threads to consider.

First and foremost, there is a difference between what are called *intrinsic* and *extrinsic* motivators. Intrinsic motivators are the ways in which an employee motivates himself. Extrinsic motivators are based more on rewarding or recognizing someone for reaching a goal of some kind. Both are important.

But it means that motivation is a two-way street. I have a two-sided book called *Walk Awhile in My Shoes*,[26] where half of the book is written from the perspective of an employee talking to a manager, and the other half of the book is written from the perspective of a manager talking to an employee. The goal of the book is to point out that both sides are dealing with unique scenarios, and things are better when both sides respect those scenarios and meet in the middle.

So how do you go about measuring what motivates each person? Similar to figuring out what characteristics different people have, you can use the data you have to create new motivation measures.

For example, suppose you want to determine which employees are motivated by leadership training. Your hunch is that people who receive leadership training are more productive. To study this, you create an attribute that identifies whether an employee has received training and another one that measures their productivity in the immediate months that follow. Your research finds that 40% of the people who received leadership training are more productive in the immediate months that follow training. So, you populate a new attribute called "Motivated by leadership training" for the 40%. The other 60% are not motivated by leadership training.

In the step where you are preparing for action, you use knowledge that approximately 35% of all training dollars go towards leadership development, with a typical cost of $3,500 per leader per year.[27] If the math shows that productivity increases by more than $3,500 per attendee, then it is worth the spend to send those 40% to formal leadership training on a regular basis. The other 60% need something else to motivate them.

If you want to see the impact that monetary rewards have on reducing turnover, then you need to create an attribute which captures who has received monetary awards and another that measures turnover. The result will yield a new attribute that suggests which employees are motivated by monetary rewards. To prepare for action, you learn that one study conducted by Saratoga Institute suggests that while 89% of managers believe most employees are pulled away by better pay, in 88% of voluntary turnovers, something besides money is the root cause.[28] Knowing this, you are not surprised to see a small number of employees who are motivated by monetary rewards.

How about the impact that a manager's transparency has on employee engagement? You need to think about a way to capture a manager's transparency and a way to measure employee engagement. Maybe you ask the employees if they know what the manager's mission is. If they don't know, there is a pretty good chance they aren't going to be too engaged. You can create an attribute out of it that tells you if manager transparency is a motivator.

My best and easiest suggestion is to get a list of motivators from a book or an article, and start there. You can always make it better and more personalized as you go. Conduct a survey with employees to find out how they would rank the list of motivators, and that should be pretty revealing.

The important thing to keep in mind is that there is not going to be a one-size-fits-all solution here. Different people will have different needs at different points in time. By linking the actions to actual business outcomes, you will begin to be able to give precise directions that produce the optimal outcome. This is what is known as *prescriptive analytics*.

Key Points

- You won't solve employee engagement and turnover issues with "programs". Each employee requires a personalized experience with their manager. If the manager is incapable of handling that responsibility, find someone else.

- Create a list of motivators using books, articles, or by interviewing and surveying employees. Manipulate the original data to come up with new motivator attributes, and connect it to the business value measures identified by you and your business leaders.

CHAPTER 7
Experimenting with Action:
The ITEM Model

Chapter 6 began with a story of how one of my bosses forced me into a "disengaged" bucket with four words delivered in a few seconds. I do not believe he set out to be a bad boss when he went to work each day. He may not have even known he was a bad boss. I was basing my judgment that he was a bad boss on my own intuition. All I kept thinking was that this leader was not aspiring to accomplish anything great. He had waved the proverbial white flag and decided that challenging the system was going to take too much effort. Only certain types of people are willing to challenge the status quo. I call them leaders. This guy was not a leader.

In thinking about the application of the DATA-INSIGHT-ACTION framework against my hunch, the simple question is: was I right? One of my favorite comedians is Mike Birbiglia. In one of his routines, he speaks of how his girlfriend gives him a hard time for being so obsessed with being right. His response: "I'm not obsessed with being right. I just am."[29]

I don't obsess with being right. I spend my days typically crunching data that either shows the facts about something historically, how something looks today, or how something is going to look by producing a forecast of some type of event. Since it is based on data, it is often right. I do obsess with making sure the DATA and INSIGHT I provide is rock solid.

When I was in graduate school, I was asked to teach the introductory statistics class in the night school. They handed me the materials that were used for the day school class that educated hundreds of students each quarter. I took one look at them, and I thought about doing it differently. I wasn't trying to be rebellious. I just happened to be a student too, so I felt that I had a data point that the teachers did not.

I asked the head of the department if I could change the organization of the course, and he gave me the OK to do so. Essentially, I flipped the course upside down. I started with the material the day school class would learn at the end of the semester, and then taught the class about the different pieces. It was sort of like doing a jigsaw puzzle. I showed them the final picture, and then we put in the right pieces.

By doing it that way, I felt the students would have a better chance of understanding *why* they were learning certain things and how it fit in the grand scheme. I used relevant examples that I thought they would relate to, rather than the examples from the textbooks. I made them collect their own data, using topics that were voted on by the class (like counting the number of beers different people in bars would consume). I just tried to keep them engaged and interested in a class topic that most of the students were forced to take.

Bottom line, it was an experiment. I had a theory that my approach would yield better results than what the day school generated. The end result was quite interesting. I gave my class the exam that was used in the day school, and 100% of my students passed the exam, most getting A's. It was only a sample of one class of about 20 students, but I had to ask myself: how was it that a graduate student had better results than people who had been trained and had many years of experience?

I wasn't totally shocked, though. My teaching experience was more about the students than it was me. I felt the best way they could learn statistics was to *experience* it, because that is what worked on me. I have the same desire for you. I want you to learn to lead better by *experiencing* what it is like to lead with data. Not just any better - quantifiably better.

Actor and comedian Ben Stein sums it up in a pretty interesting way: "Jump into the middle of things, get your hands dirty, fall flat on your face, then reach for the stars."[30] I think he is confirming that experimentation is required before you can find success.

I'm not obsessed with being right about this. I just am.

IMPROVING AND REINVENTING LEADERSHIP

Failure does not necessarily define a bad leader. But bad leaders certainly are producers of failure. Take a look at some of these statistics:[31]

- Three out of every four employees report that their boss is the worst and most stressful part of their job

- 65% of employees say they would take a new boss over a pay raise

- The amount of time it takes for an employee to shake off the stress and anxiety a bad boss causes is 22 months

- Workers that have poor relationships with bosses are 30% more likely to suffer coronary heart disease

These statistics were collected from extensive research conducted across thousands of employers. They basically suggest that most bosses are not very good, and bad ones can lead to significant personal, psychological, and even physical health issues. These are scary and expensive statistics.

Harvard Business Review stated that besides employees leaving because of their boss, they also leave due to not seeing opportunities for promotion or growth.[32] This concept ties back to the boss as well. Good bosses create opportunities for employees to shine. When their employees get promoted, they celebrate. When they don't, they think carefully about their *experience* and what they can do better. If they have data about different *experiences* from other managers, they can make wise choices about what to do next and effectively change behavior. That is what being "data-driven" is all about.

Another study suggests that a main cause of people leaving is based on "how they're doing compared with other people in their peer group, or with where they thought they would be at a certain point in life."[33] Again, I personally tie this back to the boss. A boss should recognize whether their employees are feeling like they are being mistreated or misrepresented. Again, if the boss had data that showed details of these types of comparisons, they might be able to prevent the person from leaving by addressing it.

Yet another survey indicated that people would be willing to take 15% less pay if their company simply had values like their own or shared the same purpose.[34] Another study showed that 65% of workers in North America did not receive a single word of appreciation from their boss in the last 12 months.[35]

My hunch is that none of this is too surprising if you are an HR leader. But what can you actually *do* about it? If the leadership of people were reinvented to include more of a balance of data and emotion rather than emotion by itself, the end result would be that you would be able to not only identify the best leaders in your organization, but also the best future leaders. All of your employees would be happier and more productive.

At a minimum, you could alert managers when you saw something becoming an issue based on the INSIGHT you have on these different issues. These INSIGHTS could be obtained at the organization, manager, and employee levels (at a minimum), and even by using job titles and geographic location breakouts as well.

The goal is not to automate what a manager does, but simply use the data to provide suggestions and reminders to managers so that they become better bosses and leaders. Your goal should be to give the right suggestions to your managers. This is what prescriptive analytics is all about. If you do this, then you will absolutely reinvent what leadership looks like in your organization.

The ITEM Model

The words "prescriptive analytics" should make you think about the word "prescription". When I hear "prescription", my first thought is not about analytics. It is about fixing me when I am sick. Prescriptive analytics is very similar. Its goal is to fix things when they are "sick".

If you have followed the DATA-INSIGHT-ACTION framework described in this book, you should have a quantifiable way to determine what areas of your organization are "sick". This is where INSIGHT and ACTION meet.

Pharmaceutical companies determine whether a drug is effective to treat a certain condition by conducting experiments (or in some cases, a single experiment conducted over a long period of time). Populations of interest are split into groups: one group gets the drug, and one does not. The groups receiving the drug can receive different quantities, or even different types of treatments for comparison purposes.

At the end of the experiment, the researcher evaluates the data to see if the drug did a better job of treating the illness than the other treatments (or a placebo). If they find success with statistical significance, then they can conclude that the drug is effective. But think about how a drug trial actually works. The population being tested first has to have the specific illness. In other words, if you are testing medicine that will stop headaches, then you have to have a population of people with headaches. What does that look like in workforce analytics?

You'd have to first **IDENTIFY** there is a problem to solve by using **DATA** and **INSIGHT** . You'd also need **DATA** and **INSIGHT** to **TARGET** the specific individuals that need to be helped. You'd **EXPERIMENT** with different **ACTION** in hopes of finding a way to improve or eliminate the problem. Finally, you'd **MEASURE** the value gained by improving the problem. Then you'd rinse and repeat to optimize. This four step approach, outlined in Figure 7.1, is called the ITEM model.

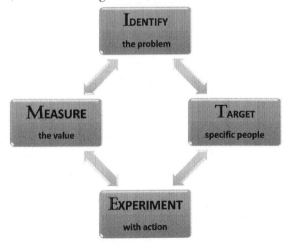

Figure 7.1: The ITEM Model

For the headache scenario, this means:

- IDENTIFY the problem: suppose data shows that 50% of people have persistent headaches, so it is a problem worth solving.

- TARGET specific people: maybe you have data that shows a cause of absenteeism being a headache, or maybe you track how many Ibuprofen tablets are taken by each employee. Or maybe you just conduct a survey and ask. Your goal is to find a sample of the people with persistent headaches (preferably using predictors or measures).

- EXPERIMENT with action: give drugs to a portion of the sample, and no drugs to the rest.

- MEASURE the value: for example, people who take drug X have 20% fewer headaches, resulting in a reduction in undesired absenteeism of 20% (which is worth ~$600 per person annually).

NOTE: this is all hypothetical data used to demonstrate the concept. Let's take a look at a real HR example.

AN EXAMPLE IN REDUCING TURNOVER

I was working with a company that felt they had a turnover problem. I used the ITEM Model to help them through each step of the process.

I first helped them measure their turnover using historical data. We found that their annual turnover had in fact been increasing over the last few years, going from about 15% to 17%. Thus, we used INSIGHT to IDENTIFY a turnover problem. I also informed them that the additional 2% of turnover increased their replacement and training costs by millions of dollars, since replacing each employee costs anywhere from 1.5x to 3x their annual salary, based on multiple studies. In their case, the additional costs were in the single-digit millions. The C-Suite was interested in the next steps as well, as everyone had something to gain.

The challenge was they didn't know what the root cause of turnover was. I asked them to conduct an experiment by providing a simple survey to their managers to rate whether each of their direct reports was at risk of leaving their organization. My goal was two-fold: primarily, the goal was to TARGET the employees that were most likely to leave so we could ACT. Secondarily, though, I wanted to see if the managers were any good at answering this question.

The results of the survey showed that only about 2% of the employees were identified as being high risk of leaving. Of course, since the company's *actual* annual turnover rate was closer to 17%, there was clearly some "sickness" going on.

Two very important INSIGHTS came out of this first little experiment: first, managers did a poor job at TARGETING employees who were likely to leave; and second, their managers/bosses really did not have a good gauge on how to identify turnover risk. The difference is subtle - one is identifying people, and the other is identifying the cause. The general consensus was that this company had more bad bosses than they ever thought.

But there was another piece of the puzzle to consider. Just because the managers said certain employees were a high risk of leaving, we still didn't know if those people actually *were* the ones that were leaving. In other words, how good were the managers' predictions? We monitored them for the next 12 months.

Remember how to measure chance:

	Event happens	Event doesn't happen
You predict an event	You got it right (True positive)	You guessed wrong (False positive)
You predict a non-event	You guessed wrong (False negative)	You got it right (True negative)

$$\text{Chance} = \frac{\textit{How many times did you guess right?}}{\textit{How many guesses did you make?}}$$

The results showed that about 40% of the group that the managers identified as high risk of leaving actually left. So, we filled in the box with the results. Let's walk through how we filled in each box.

To fill in the "You got it right" box in the upper left corner, we had to think about the number of employees that the managers guessed would leave (2%) and the number that actually left (40% of that group). Thus, to fill in this first box, we multiplied 40% and 2%. The end result is that less than 1% of the employees were correct TARGETS.

	Employees left	Employees did not leave
Managers predicted they would leave	40% of 2% = 0.8%	
Managers predicted they would stay		

Next, we'll filled in the "You guessed wrong (false positive)" box. We knew that managers predicted 2% of people would leave, so filling in this box is merely the difference between 2% and 0.8% (from the first box).

	Employees left	Employees did not leave
Managers predicted they would leave	40% of 2% = 0.8%	2% - 0.8% = 1.2%
Managers predicted they would stay		

Next, we filled in the "You guessed wrong (false negative)" box. We knew that 17% of employees left, so this box was just the difference between 17% and 0.8%,

	Employees left	Employees did not leave
Managers predicted they would leave	40% of 2% = 0.8%	2% - 0.8% = 1.2%
Managers predicted they would stay	17% - 0.8% = 16.2%	

Finally, we filled in the "You guessed right" in the lower left corner. Since 17% left, it means that 83% did not leave. Thus, the bottom right box is the difference between 83% and 1.2%.

	Employees left	Employees did not leave
Managers predicted they would leave	40% of 2% = 0.8%	2% - 0.8% = 1.2%
Managers predicted they would stay	17% - 0.8% = 16.2%	83% - 1.2% = 81.8%

So, managers guessed right 82.6% of the time (0.8% + 81.8%). Not terrible.

But, a closer look reveals that the managers did a good job of guessing when someone would stay, but not so good at guessing when they would leave. The managers correctly identified less than 5% of all of the turnover that occurred (0.8% ÷ 17% = 4.7%). Not so good. But for the records they identified, we now had a quantifiable measure of the current state of the manager's ability to identify turnover. 4.7% of turnover in 2% of the population, or 2.35x (4.7% ÷ 2% = 235%) better than random. Not so bad.

At the same time they conducted the survey, I had an additional experiment for them to consider. Specifically, we created a statistical model to predict which employees were likely to leave. Since 100% of the employees were scored, I suggested they only monitor the 10% of employees who had the highest likelihood of leaving based on the data. Similar to the survey-based approach, we also monitored those employees for 12 months.

The results showed that about 60% of the group that the predictive analytics identified as high risk of leaving actually left. Again, we can fill in the box with the results:

	Employees left	Employees did not leave
Model predicted they would leave	60% of 10% = 6.0%	10% - 6% = 4.0%
Model predicted they would stay	17% - 6.0% = 11.0%	83% - 4.0% = 79.0%

The data guessed the right outcome 85.0% of the time (6.0% + 79.0%). This is a better result than the managers got.

More importantly, the predictive analytics approach identified 35% of the entire turnover that occurred (6% ÷ 17% = 35.3%). We now had a quantifiable measure of the current state of the data-driven identifier. 35.3% of turnover in 10% of the population, or 3.53x (35.3% ÷ 10% = 353%) better than random.

It is pretty easy to see that the data-driven approach (3.53x) provided a much better result than the manager hunch (2.35x). I told the company that a retention program applied only to the riskiest 10% of employees could reduce the turnover by up to 35%, and the cost savings would also be up to 35%, which for this company was in the tens of millions of dollars. The alternative of relying on manager judgment might reduce overall turnover by 5%, but the savings would be much less - probably under one million dollars.

But there was even an additional piece of INSIGHT that we found as well. Because the managers had TARGETS on so few people, the chances of the two approaches putting TARGETS on the same people were pretty small. I don't want to get into probability analysis too much, but the chances of a person being TARGETED with both approaches (assuming independence) is 2% x 10% = 0.2%. In fact, the actual number of people targeted by both could be counted on one hand.

Since the overlap was so small, and the success of the managers was decent, I suggested they use both groups in their retention program. In other words, the combined approaches would identify 35.3% + 4.7% = 40.0% of the turnover in only 12% of the people. That is a nice return.

It was scary to think they could do a program like this and ignore the other 60% of people, but I used INSIGHT to show them that their return on any investment on those employees was a waste of money.

Let's evaluate how we followed the ITEM Model:

1. IDENTIFY the problem: Turnover had increased from 15% to 17% over the past few years.

2. TARGET specific people:

    a. the Managers were given a survey to identify which employees they thought were at high risk of leaving (TARGET based on opinion).

    b. Predictive analytics were also leveraged to see how many employees were at high risk of leaving (TARGET based on data).

3. EXPERIMENT with ACTION: One experiment was to determine if managers' opinions were stronger than predictive analytics. The experiment showed that while both were good, predictive analytics identified significantly more high-risk candidates at a higher accuracy.

4. MEASURE the value:

    a. Company identified that they could reduce turnover by up to 40% by applying a program on only 12% of the people. Assuming a 50% success rate, the company could quantify savings in the tens of millions of dollars.

Since they had a good story, the next step was to go back to EXPERIMENT and come up with action plans to save the specific TARGETs.

As you might imagine, we were able to break through a lot of barriers since we based everything on data points and the right analytics.

Key Points

- To improve and reinvent leadership, you are going to have to be prepared to experiment in order to find the optimal path to change.

- Follow the ITEM Model to achieve the best results. Memorize what each letter means:

    I for IDENTIFY the problem

    T for TARGET specific people

    E for EXPERIMENT with action

    M for MEASURE the value.

CHAPTER 8
Watch Out For These Things

If you've followed all of the guidance provided in *Quantifiably Better*, you are probably feeling like you just earned a degree in Industrial and Organizational Psychology, and possibly Business Analytics. In some regards, you have.

I-O Psychology is the study of human behavior in the workplace, while Business Analytics is all about studying the business data in an organization, especially through the usage of statistical techniques. The role of the HR leader is to bridge this gap. That is, to change people's behavior so that better business outcomes are generated.

But there is a secondary and more personal purpose that I think we also share. We both want to make people's lives quantifiably better.

We like to focus on others. We put our own causes last. Helping others brings us great joy. When we marry our work to this personal journey, it develops an amazing camaraderie that excites us to the core.

Everything can be improved. That is why we measure things. We use our creativity to find more optimal solutions, even when the current scenario is pretty good. We can measure the effectiveness of new solutions, and when they work, it is a thrilling moment.

However, whether you are just getting started on your people analytics journey, or you are already underway, you are likely to run into a few different scenarios. To improve your chances of success, on the following pages are five principles that cover situations that can be obstacles along your journey.

SHOW ONLY THE THINGS YOU NEED

It may surprise you that my life is not one big dashboard of metrics. I try to measure things as often as possible, especially the less obvious things. But it isn't essential for my survival. What is essential in my day-to-day activities is the following statement:

An analytic without action is useless.

This is an important principle to consider. Much like the earlier chapter where "analysis paralysis" was discussed, it is very easy to fall into a trap where you have more metrics than you can react to. Whether you believe the theory that the brain can only handle 5-9 things at a given point in time or not, I can tell you from experience that showing more than you need will only create additional questions. Less is more in this case.

I mentioned in an earlier chapter that it is important to prepare for ACTION before you start to show off your newfound INSIGHT. That logic is where this principle comes into play. The solution is simple: separate what you measure, from what you measure *and* propose to act upon. You can easily have metrics available on thousands of data points, but only show people the metrics that you can connect to the requirement to take immediate action.

Doing this will allow you to hold others accountable. There is nothing more frustrating that showing a room full of people important INSIGHT only for them to walk away not knowing what to do next. Tie your analytics to action.

TURN SMALL STUFF INTO BIG STUFF

As you begin to measure more and more things, especially with data quality and the seven C's, you undoubtedly will find metrics that although are very small, require attention.

This leads to another principle:

Never care about less than 1% of anything.

Don't get me wrong. I'm not at all questioning the importance of the 1%. I'm simply saying that it will be more difficult to get people excited to change their behavior over something very small. It will be equally difficult to create excitement by measuring the small number over and over again.

The solution to this is to pair the original small metric with another. In other words, instead of showing that less than 1% of people have a characteristic, show how this small population impacts something that is bigger than 1%, like bottom line, or costs.

For example, telling your audience that you can reduce turnover by 0.5% is not as effective as telling them that reducing turnover by 0.5% will cause a savings of one million dollars. Pairing the small metric with a larger one will capture the appropriate attention.

It is equally important not to measure the same thing a hundred different ways. Just find one way to connect the small metric to a bigger one.

PASSION AND INCENTIVES

In terms of describing employee passion, it typically means that the employee so strongly believes in something that it almost consumes them. Employers want their employees to be passionate towards their cause, and at times they can achieve this. Passion is contagious.

If you are passionate towards using data to change human behavior, then you are way more likely to find partners in the business who share your passion.

However, as time passes, the flame will likely start to burn out on whatever data-driven initiative you kick off. The managers and employees may see an early positive result, and as a result be very passionate about continuing. But over time, this passion will dwindle.

One common way to deal with this loss of interest is to incentivize data-driven initiatives in some way, be it monetary or by some other type of reward. This is a very reasonable approach, but it leads to another important principle:

When you see the passion draining, do not rely on incentives.

Think of the way that one trains a dog to come when one calls it. At first, you provide a treat every time. Over time, you provide a treat every other time, and then with even further gaps, until eventually, they come whenever you call even when there is no treat. They will keep coming because maybe this time, there will be a treat.

This is truly how behavior modification should work. You are likely to need some incentives to get people interested, but sustained change is only accomplished when incentives are no longer required, or are at least more random.

In a study conducted in the 1970's called "The Hidden Costs of Rewards"[36], preschoolers were asked to draw pictures, but they were first broken out into three groups. One group was told they were going to receive incentives. A second group received incentives without knowledge. The third did not receive any incentive at all. What the researchers found was that the group that was told about the incentives actually became less interested in drawing over time, while the other two groups stayed motivated to draw. The children in the first group lost their passion because it was too strongly tied to incentives.

In practice, incentives can force people to be motivated, but over time, the incentives need to be more random in nature, so that the receipt is always exciting. Motivation is a critical component of keeping people passionate. So you will have to find ways to motivate them without incentives as well.

THE SHINY CAR SCENARIO

As you go down the DATA-INSIGHT-ACTION path, you are likely to encounter a great deal of success, especially early in the journey. You will be revealing things about employees to their leaders or themselves for the first time. The newness of the information will be enough to capture people's interests. Their mouths might drop to the floor in their excitement about a new learning. But, the metrics are not likely to change dramatically. If you show updated results to someone, and the results are essentially the same, they are not likely to be too impressed, and they may start to lose interest.

This scenario is very similar to the experience one has when buying a new car. When you first drive it, you are incredibly excited, and you want to show it off to others. They may even share in your excitement. However, as the days go by, the new car starts to become less exciting. It still requires maintenance, and the glossy coat starts to lose its sheen. The cool new features you were so proud of are now part of every car. After a while, someone else buys a new car that pulls the attention away from you.

You should expect this to happen with your analytical journey, too.

Showing people a new analytic is the equivalent of a shiny new car: exciting at first, but unstimulating later.

Knowing you are going to create a lot of excitement at the beginning will be your best chance at personal recognition. To maintain the recognition, you are going to have to continue to generate new analytics all the time. Otherwise, you will just be driving the same old car. Just keep thinking that each new metric that you can tie to action will be just like the team getting a new, shiny car.

In practice, you might consider showing two new metrics for every existing one. That will keep people interested for a longer time.

SETTING GOALS FOR OTHERS

Your job as the analytics expert is to consult, not to control. If people feel forced to do things, even though you can mathematically prove they might be wildly successful, they may become resentful towards participating.

When you show people analytics for the first time, your goal should not be to control the situation, but to get *them* to control the situation. This leads to another principle:

If you strike gold, shut up.

A former boss and mentor said those words to me in describing what happens when you want someone else to take charge. As they start to agree with you (i.e. when you "strike gold"), the wrong thing to do is to start directing right away. Let them talk and figure it out. Steer them towards the right answer, but you don't have to be the one to point it out. If you've done things right, you will have an answer to their next question.

Keep in mind that the audience is likely seeing the metric for the first time, while you have had ample time to become the expert. In other words, by design, they won't understand it as well as you do. Be prepared to tell your story and proposal for action repeatedly - maybe dozens of times. Patience will be an important virtue.

Goals that others set for you can be significant de-motivators, but goals that people set for themselves are healthy.[37] The more you get the leaders, managers, and employees to set the goals for themselves, the more they will feel a drive to meet them. To get this result, you will likely have to do twice as much listening as talking. Your ability to influence others to own the goals you want met will be highly correlated with how well they think you understand their needs.

Stephen Covey describes this phenomenon very well in the fifth habit of *The Seven Habits of Highly Effective People* by saying that people should seek first to understand, and then be understood.[38] You will have to learn how to listen carefully, and then learn to be persuasive. You want to lead the horse to water, but leave it up to the horse to drink when he understands that the water will quench his thirst.

Key Points

- "An analytic without action is useless." Show only what is immediately actionable.

Key Points (continued)

- "Never care about less than 1% of anything." Pair small numbers with larger ones to increase impact.

- "When you see the passion beginning to drain, do not rely on incentives completely." Incentives are OK to initiate changes in behavior, but over time, they should be more random and periodic.

- "Showing people a new analytic is the equivalent of showing them your new car: exciting at first, but unstimulating later." Keep inventing new metrics to keep people interested.

- "If you strike gold, shut up." Listen twice as much as you talk, and know that you can only influence those who feel they are understood.

CHAPTER 9
Everything Can Be Quantifiably Better

As I have gained professional, emotional, spiritual, physical, social, nutritional, intellectual, and financial experience, I have concluded one thing:

Everything and everyone can be made quantifiably better.

I was recently sitting at the airport, and I was watching the people go by. I started to wonder what kinds of professional and personal challenges each person was dealing with. I thought about how each person has some unique combination of data points that tell about all of the categories I mentioned above.

I didn't just stop there. I started to think about the people around them - their bosses, peers, subordinates, customers, friends, spouses, children, family members, or maybe even the people they are passing while walking down the airport corridor. I wondered which people had the greatest positive and negative impacts in their lives, and I considered whether there could be patterns within those answers.

I thought about each of the situations in their lives that cause them stress or anxiety in any way, and how those stresses and anxieties were impacting those around them. Was their marriage good? Were they married at all? Were their kids dealing with something big? Were they in physical or emotional pain? Were they struggling financially? Did they have the right job?

I thought about their individual days and how the stuff that was happening around them could be impacting them. They burned their tongue on their coffee this morning. Their grocery store stopped carrying their favorite product. They need to eat. Their car needs gas. The news reported another terrorist attack. Traffic to work was abysmal. Their competitor just stole some business. The dog needs a bath.

I watched their facial expressions tell a story. I listened to the tones of their voices, some talking on the phone in really loud voices, some quietly. Some of them were talking to people they knew, and some were talking to people they clearly did not know. Some were texting and walking, while others were frantically looking for a place to charge their phones. Some just looked lost, both literally and figuratively. I saw overweight people, physically fit people, people with limps, people who walked fast, people who walked slow, people who couldn't walk at all.

Their appearances alone told stories in my head. I jokingly started to think, "this is how fiction writers come up with stories", and wondered if any of them had ever written or tried writing. I saw some of them were musicians, and I wondered if they wrote their own songs and lyrics, and if so, could I determine their personality type from what they wrote about? Was there a trend in the types of lyrics they wrote today versus a year ago?

I was overwhelmed with these thoughts. Every single one of these things I thought about was a data point that could be captured in some way. Some would be easy to capture, and others would have to be defined with the "stake in the ground" approach. I was solving the problem in my head as I observed it.

I started to have some doubtful thoughts enter into my mind, as I began to wonder if I was, as Solomon said in the Bible, "chasing the wind" in my efforts to measure people in some meaningful way. But then, more importantly, I started to think about the outcomes that were possible, and I brought it all back to one simple thought.

I thought: "man, all of these people could be quantifiably better."

You know, like most people think when they are at the airport.

I recognize that it isn't practical to collect all of the data points about a person. Not ever. But I can certainly use the data that I have to measure things and make predictive guesses on what will happen next. The more data points I have, the better the guesses will be.

But a smarter guess is no different than a hunch. It is why I stress over and over the importance of tying the analytics to action.

This entire book is all about adding a little insight and knowledge about people into our brains. Once we have that knowledge, we can make very targeted choices about how to make even the slightest changes. Compare the results of time A to time B to see if improvement occurred. If it did, repeat, or try something else. If not, try something else anyway. Eventually, something will be measurably different in a positive way.

I have done my best to provide how-to instructions on how to get started, as well as next steps for those that are somewhere downstream already. I think the best way to conclude the book is with a potential project plan that you can execute and share with your leaders. I assure you that you have data in your possession that nobody else on the planet has, but you just need to think about how to use it. Otherwise, I'd challenge you as to why you are collecting it in the first place.

It's time for action.

THE PROJECT PLAN

I am hopeful that the last eight chapters were explained in such a way that you feel armed and ready to take on the challenge of bringing or accelerating the usage of data and analytics to help manage your workforce.

In the following pages, you will find a general roadmap that you can publish into your own presentations to senior leaders, as well as a flowchart to help you decipher what happens each step of the way with the expected deliverables. You don't need to present it all at once - you have a long-term game plan about which you can explain and sound knowledgeable.

Having this all in one place is very beneficial to ensuring that you are able to execute on the strategy and not just talk about it. Execution means everything.

The Project Plan

Step 1:

Create a presentation describing the vision you have for a data-driven organization. Be sure to explain that you will be tying the vision to the business problems and outcomes the C-suite cares about most.

Introduce the concept of DATA - INSIGHT - ACTION. Explain that you have a plan to get through all of it, beginning with gaining expertise on the data.

Explain how you will use the 7 C's to familiarize yourself with the quality of the data. State that the data isn't perfect, and that those imperfections will be improved over time once there are measures in place.

Explain that your first set of deliverables will be reports on the 7 C's, and that these reports will feed into an overall scorecard. You may need to break it out by organization to appease your C-suite partners.

Explain how you will use the Data & Insight Maturity Model to prepare to solve the problems that the C-suite cares about most. You will be creating meaningful attributes that you will correlate to the outcomes, and you will monitor them closely. You will also start to think about how you will be rolling out your new solution and strategy, not guaranteeing results, but acknowledging that you are going to do something.

Explain that you will use the ITEM model for setting up appropriate experiments so that you will see the effectiveness of the personalized actions. Explain that these will not broadly target everyone, but strict populations that have been identified using data.

Finally, explain that you will measure the effectiveness of the experiments by tying the outcomes back to the measures that the C-suite uses.

If you need help, this is time to ask for funding for an intern, or at least partner with your IT department (or any of your analytics departments, if you are fortunate enough to have at least one). You should feel confident in your business case; your funding arms will see that confidence, and they will at least consider giving you what you need.

Give yourself a realistic time frame, and deliver the first set of metrics. Be sure you have no more than 5-9 slides of metrics in total (since the brain can only handle 5-9 things at any one time), but feel free to have an appendix full of as many metrics as you create.

Step 2:

Now that you have a grasp of the quality of the data you are working with, it is time to create some new attributes. Find a professional leadership book you (or one of your C-suite partners) enjoy.

Hold a brainstorming session with a goal of creating no more than 10 attributes from the leadership book, preferably by manipulating the data you have. Let the teams figure out how to define the new attributes if possible, so they will claim some ownership, but also feel like they are participating in the solution.

Run these new attributes through the 7 C's. See if there is any correlation with any of the key business issues and outcomes the C-suite identified. If you strike gold, share the metrics.

Have a realistic time frame, but keep the window as short as possible. This is your chance for a quick win.

Step 3:

It's time to start monitoring the data. Set up your control limits (you should have a little history of the data quality statistics at this point).

Make sure the reports are running automatically (hands-off), but sending notifications via email to you when an attribute is outside of a control limit. You may have to adjust the control limits if there are too many or too few notifications.

Step 4:

Hold another brainstorming session where you will define the specific business problem you want to explore and solve. Turnover is an easy one to begin with, but be sure that you tie your goal of reducing turnover to real business outcomes. For instance, replacing a person costs 1.5x - 3x their annual salary. Use average salaries to explain what the impact of saving as few as 10 people will be. If you choose a different topic, be sure to tie the outcome to a metric that is important to the C-suite, especially where money or productivity is involved.

Create or leverage a report that shows the financial/productivity metric that is desired, and explain that success will be defined by that metric.

Use the Data & Insight Maturity Model to figure out where you are starting, and then set a realistic goal of where you hope the results will end up. Keep in mind that if your target is to improve something by less than 1%, your goal should be in dollars. You don't need to explain "how" you will get there just yet. This step is all about getting aligned.

Step 5:

Once you have buy-in, hold another brainstorming session where you will define at least 10 possible actions that you wish to evaluate. Consider focusing on motivators, as people will change their behavior if you motivate them in the way they need.

Use the ITEM model to identify the problem, determine how you will target the specific individuals that will be acted upon (make sure you have a way to record the action in your data too), run the experiment, and measure the outcome. Consider whether or not you need incentives to gain participation.

If you reached your goals, celebrate like crazy. Explain to your C-suite partners that your data-driven approach was successful. Show no more than 3 slides of before and after metrics. Explain that things are quantifiably better, just as you promised. Have supporting metrics handy in an appendix or Business Intelligence system.

If you did not reach your goals, celebrate like crazy, because you just figured out 10 actions that you no longer will leverage since they did not have the desired impact. Come up with 10 more, or select a different problem. It may be appropriate to offer better incentives if participation was low.

Remind everyone that you are monitoring the quality of the data, and if there any specific departments that are seeing bad trends, point out that the leaders need to own and improve the metrics. Offer them an incentive if they reach certain goals.

Step 6:

Over time, you will be able to create predictive and prescriptive analytics based on the actions recorded. You will be able to suggest the right actions for a manager/employee to take over time.

Consider hiring someone with a statistics or data science background to help lead the effort.

Keep creating new reports and analytics constantly, but limit what you show to your C-suite partners. Never more than 3 new reports in any one setting to avoid "analysis paralysis."

For your own usage, you can use this simple table to remind you of your ongoing journey:

DATA	INSIGHT	ACTION
Quality - Seven C's (Chapter 2)		
Manipulate (Chapter 3)		
Monitor (Chapter 4)		
The Data & Analytics Maturity Model (Chapter 5) REPORT MANIPULATE MONITOR PREPARE for ACTION		
Motivators (Chapter 6)		
The ITEM Model (Chapter 7) IDENTIFY the problem TARGET specific individuals EXPERIMENT with action MEASURE the value		
Principles: An analytic without action is useless Never care about less than 1% of anything When you see the passion draining, do not rely on incentives Showing people a new analytic is the equivalent of a shiny new car: exciting at first, but unstimulating later If you strike gold, shut up		

Figure 9.1: A reminder of your ongoing journey

The Final Step

Take a deep breath. If you made it this far, then you are now a data-driven HR leader. You are (hopefully) monitoring all of the areas that used to keep you up at night. That should be *one less thing* about which to worry.

One less thing. Such a simple concept.

Key Points

- Everything and everyone can be quantifiably better.

- Use the Project Plan to initiate the right conversations with your leadership team. You don't have to present all of this at once - it gives you several years' worth of material.

References

Chapter 1

1 - Starkey, S., Tisch, S., & Finerman, W. (Producers) & Zemeckis, R. (Director). (1994). *Forrest Gump* [Motion picture]. United States: Paramount Pictures.

2 - Davenport, T. H., & Patil, D. (2012, October). *Data Scientist: The Sexiest Job of The 21st Century.* Harvard Business Review.

3 - Weller, C. (2015, February 25). *Human Brain Adapts To Modern Problem-Solving With Skills Learned Through Evolution.* Retrieved August 16, 2016, from http://www.medicaldaily.com/human-brain-adapts-modern-problem-solving-skills-learned-through-evolution-323464.

4 - Kelvin, W. T. (1889). *Popular lectures and addresses.* London: Macmillan and Co.

5 - Silverman, R. E. (2012, September 20). *Big Data Upends the Way Workers Are Paid.* The Wall Street Journal.

6 - Carroll, G. (Producer) & Rosenberg, S. (Director). (1967). *Cool Hand Luke* [Motion picture]. United States: Warner Bros.-Seven Arts.

7 - Hopkins, A. (n.d.). *Famous Quotes at BrainyQuote.* Retrieved 2016 from http://www.brainyquote.com.

Chapter 2

8 - Gardner, C., & Rivas, M. E. (2009). Start Where You Are: Life Lessons In Getting From Where You Are To Where You Want To Be. New York: Amistad.

9 - Canfield, J., & Switzer, J. (2005). The Success Principles: How To Get From Where You Are To Where You Want To Be. New York: Harper Resource Book.

Chapter 3

10 - Retrieved 2016 from http://www.dictionary.com.

11 - Buckingham, M., & Clifton, D. O. (2001). *Now, Discover Your Strengths.* New York: Free Press.

12 - Barksdale, J. (n.d.). *Quotable Quotes at GoodReads.* Retrieved 2016 from http://www.goodreads.com.

13 - Mayer, J. D. (2014). *Personal Intelligence: The Power of Personality and How it Shapes Our Lives.* New York: Scientific American/Farrar, Straus and Giroux.

Chapter 4

14 - Stein, G. (1975). Reflection on the Atomic Bomb (The Previously Uncollected Writings of Gertrude Stein, Volume I). Black Sparrow Press.

15 - *Inspirational Stories, Quotes & Poems | Inspirational Short Stories.* (n.d.). Retrieved 2016 from http://www.inspirationalstories.com/.

Chapter 5

16 - Belson, K. & Hartwell, J. (Producers) & DeMicco, K. & Sanders, C. (Directors). (2013). *The Croods* [Motion picture]. United States: DreamWorks Animation.

17 - Robbins, A. (1986). *Unlimited power: The new science of personal achievement.* New York: Simon and Schuster.

18 - Miller, G. A. (1956). The Magical Number Seven, Plus or Minus Two: Some Limits on Our Capacity for Processing Information. Psychological Review, 63, 81-97.

19 - Gladwell, M. (2008). *Outliers: The story of success.* New York: Little, Brown and Co.

20 - Rohn, J. (n.d.). *Famous Quotes at BrainyQuote.* Retrieved 2016 from http://www.brainyquote.com.

Chapter 6

21 - Graves, S. R. (n.d.). *How to Achieve Greatness.* Retrieved 2016 from http://www.stephenrgraves.com/articles/read/how-to-forge-greatness/.

22 - Gallup. (2016). *The Worldwide Employee Engagement Crisis.* Retrieved 2016 from http://www.gallup.com/businessjournal/188033/worldwide-employee-engagement-crisis.aspx.

23 - Lipman, V. (2015). The Type B manager: Leading successfully in a type A world. Prentice Hall Press.

24 - Hall, K. (n.d.). *5 Takeaways from BenchmarkPro 2016.* Retrieved 2016 from http://blog.compdatasurveys.com/2016-benchmarkpro-results-now-available.

25 - *Job Openings and Labor Turnover Survey News Release.* (n.d.). Retrieved 2016, from http://www.bls.gov/news.release/archives/jolts_03172016.htm.

26 - Harvey, E., & Ventura, S. (1996). Walk awhile in my shoes: Gut-level, real-world messages from employees to managers. Dallas, TX: Performance Pub.

27 - McCann, D. (2014, March 14). *Leadership Development Is Top Human-Capital Need: Deloitte.* Retrieved 2016 from

http://ww2.cfo.com/leadership/2014/03/developing-leaders-hrs-important-function/.

28 - Branham, L. (2005). The 7 hidden reasons employees leave: How to recognize the subtle signs and act before it's too late. eNew York: American Management Association.

Chapter 7

29 - Birbiglia, M. (Writer), & Barrish, S. (Director). (2013). *My Girlfriend's Boyfriend* [Motion picture on DVD]. United States: New Wave Entertainment Television.

30 - Stein, B. (n.d.). *Ben Stein Quotes*. Retrieved 2017 from https://www.brainyquote.com/quotes/quotes/b/benstein119110. html.

31 - Ouimet, M. (2012). *The Real Productivity-Killer: Jerks*. Retrieved October 28, 2016 from http://www.inc.com/maeghan-ouimet/real-cost-bad-bosses.html.

32 - *Why People Quit Their Jobs*. (2016). Retrieved 2016 from https://hbr.org/2016/09/why-people-quit-their-jobs.

33 - *The New Path Forward - CEMLA*. (2016, April). Retrieved 2016 from http://www.cemla.org/actividades/2016/2016-04-RecursosHumanos/2016-04-RecursosHumanos4.pdf.

34 - Zukin, C., & Szeltner, M. (2012). *Talent Report: What Workers Want in 2012 - Net Impact*. Retrieved October 31, 2016, from https://netimpact.org/sites/default/files/documents/what-workers-want-2012.pdf.

35 - Tanner, O.C. *Performance: Accelerated*. (n.d.). Retrieved 2016 from http://www.octanner.com/content/dam/oc-tanner/documents/white-papers/Performance-Accelerated-Whitepaper.pdf.

Chapter 8

36 - Lepper, M. R., & Greene, D. (1978). *The Hidden Costs of Reward: New Perspectives on the Psychology of Human Motivation.* Hillsdale, NJ: L. Erlbaum Associates.

37 - Ordóñez, L. D., Schweitzer, M. E., Galinsky, A. D., & Bazerman, M. H. (2009). *Goals gone wild: The systematic side effects of over-prescribing goal setting.* Boston: Harvard Business School.

38 - Covey, S. R. (1989). The seven habits of highly effective people: Restoring the character ethic. New York: Simon and Schuster.

Index

Made in the USA
Columbia, SC
05 February 2019